WHAT IS THE CHRISTIAN ORIENT?

IGNACE DICK

What
Is the Christian
Orient?

Translated by C. GERARD GUERTIN

The Newman Press · Westminster, Maryland

1967

The present volume is a translation of QU'EST-CE QUE L'ORIENT
CHRÉTIEN? published in French in 1965 by Casterman, Tournai, Bel-
gium. © 1965 Casterman.

Nihil obstat: Martinus S. Rushford, Ph.D.
    Censor librorum

Imprimatur: Bryan Josephus McEntegart, D.D.
    Archiepiscopus-Episcopus Bruklyniensis
    August 23, 1966

  The *Nihil obstat* and *Imprimatur* are official declarations that a
book or pamphlet is free of doctrinal or moral error. No implication is
contained therein that those who have granted the *Nihil obstat* and
Imprimatur agree with the opinions expressed. Copyright © 1967 by
THE MISSIONARY SOCIETY OF SAINT PAUL THE APOSTLE in the State
of New York. *Library of Congress Catalog Card Number:* 66-28936.
Printed in the United States of America.

CONTENTS

INTRODUCTION

O NE OF THE GREAT misfortunes of the Middle Ages was the breakdown of Roman influence. It was not long after this fracture in the old civilization that the unity of the Church felt its influence. Each section of the Old World lived henceforth apart. The diversities which, until then, had coexisted in unity were changed into oppositions; each section made an absolute of its own tradition and did not recognize the legitimate personality of the other.

The see of Rome should have been the bond of unity, but it was too much part of the Western world. Its universal authority of divine right, moreover, was not entirely accepted in the East. As a result, the two portions of the Church lived from then on as strangers to one another.

Today we are witnessing a phenomenon of universalization analogous to that of the Roman Empire. Western civilization is no longer considered to be the whole of civilization, as history is being written on a planetary scale. The countries of the Near and Middle East are now looked upon by Europe not as countries to be exploited or protected, but as countries to be reckoned with and treated as equals. Europe welcomes the values of other cultures. Thus it is that we rediscover the necessary climate of

mutual understanding, respect and esteem for one another
—a first step towards sharing a common life again.

Yet, despite the repeated appeals of recent popes, especially of Leo XIII and Pius XI, the enlightened interest
in the Christian Orient is far from penetrating the inner
circles of the clergy or of the Christian people of the West.

Today, a real effort is underway. This book is directed to
those who sympathize more and more with the East. Its
object is to present the Christian Orient as it is, to high-
light its originality in relation to the West, and to situate
it within the Universal Church.

The first part will be devoted principally to describing
that phenomenon which is Oriental Christianity. The second part will try to discover its values and its meaning,
before taking on the problem of the split and the reunion
of the two portions of Christendom.

WHAT IS THE CHRISTIAN ORIENT?

PART I · TO KNOW THE ORIENT

THERE ARE MANY "Christian Orients." There is the Orient of the archeologists and of the philologists, a world where many erudite scholars live. After the fifteenth century the Orient lost its appeal for them because it ceased to be the vestige of the Christian past; it was nothing more than a cultural reality, not a human world which lives and evolves. This Orient still exists in the universities of Europe and America.

There is the Orient known to the tourists and the journalists, an Orient such as might appear to a visitor from the moon, cut off from its historical and cultural roots. This Orient appears to be very complex. At times charming and curious, it enchants some pilgrims to the Holy Land, but its importance in the Universal Church, in the final analysis, is negligible. This Orient can be found in a travel prospectus and on advertising stickers displayed by pilgrims or missionaries.

But no amount of reporting, no matter how detailed or exhaustive, can give an accurate picture of the real Christian Orient. This one can be understood only in the light of its history and its culture, because it crystallizes nineteen centuries of Christian history. Neither can it be treated merely as historians do, in the manner of the classic philologists. If the Christian Orient actually reflects all of the Christian past, it lives and confronts all modern realities.

Our historical exploration, therefore, will attempt to discover the meaning of existing realities as values and as lifelines. We shall not limit ourselves to any one particular aspect of the Orient—rites, church-communities and ethnic minorities—but shall endeavor to consider the Christian Orient as a whole reality, as Church and at the same time as Christendom.

GEOGRAPHY OF THE CHRISTIAN ORIENT

Since the earth is round, its division into East and West might appear to be somewhat arbitrary. Yet we say that the United States is east of the Far Eastern countries. There are however an Orient and an Occident which represent cultural more than they do geographic realities. If we use the center of our Old World as our point of reference, Marrakesh is an oriental, and Sydney, an occidental city, since the first of these cities belongs to a civilization which came from the geographic East, whereas the second came from a civilization which developed in the West.

The Christian Orient is not to be found in the churches of Japan, nor among the Latins of Greece or of Jerusalem, because these Christian communities are affiliates of the Western Church. It is the one whose religious way of life comes from a direct line of churches in eastern regions of the Roman Empire, Asia-Minor, Syria and Egypt, that is, churches of Apostolic origin which do not look to Rome for their birth, their growth or their organization.

This Orient reaches into Poland, Czechoslovakia and southern Italy; it encompasses eastern Europe, western Asia and north-east Africa; its southern extremities reach into Ethiopia and Malabar, in the south of India. This far-reaching territory is made up of two distinct zones. According to the description of Father Rondot, the Christians in the European section always appear in concentrated groups where Christianity has impregnated the national culture; the Christians in the Afro-Asian zone appear as islands or blocks emerging from a Moslem sea like a vast archipelago, the remnants of a broken continent. These two geographic zones correspond to the two Eastern political blocks of the Middle Ages, the Byzantine Empire and the Arabian Empire, each with its own sphere of influence.

The regions conquered by the Arabs, namely, Egypt, Syria, Mesopotamia, Persia, were precisely the areas of the Orient which were little effected by Hellenism. Here, Greek quickly disappeared as the cultural language because this was now the domain of Syriac, of Coptic, of Armenian, of Georgian, of Ethiopian and of Arabic. This division of Greek Asia Minor dates back to the end of the Middle Ages and is due mainly to the influx of the Turkish tribes.

A theological cleavage corresponded to the cultural. While the Greco-Slavonic World under Byzantine domination adhered to the Orthodoxy of the first seven councils, the majority of Oriental Christians under Arabian domination reflected the christological theses condemned by the fifth-century councils, such as Nestorianism, Monophysitism, and Monothelitism. The only exceptions were the Melkites of Syria and Egypt, who in the midst of the Arabian Empire still maintained their ties with Orthodoxy. During the Middle Ages they were in the minority and inhabited the very sections of Syria and Egypt, that is, western Syria and northern Egypt, which were the most Hellenized. Inevitably the theological differences would blend with the ethnic and cultural realities, and the political divergencies would later make them stronger.[1]

Hence, the Christian Orient can be divided into two clearly identified zones: We find there the European Greco-Slavonic zone, compact, administratively divided into autonomous and homogeneous national churches, but enjoying a clear liturgical unity in the Byzantine rite and dogmatic unity in Orthodoxy. The only indication of variation remained in the language—Greek or Slavonic, notably: Rumanian. We cannot predict whether the Iron Curtain, which limits the Greco-Slavonic frontier, will further solidify these differences. We also find the Afro-Asian zone submerged to a great extent in Islamism, divided into several liturgical and confessional groups which transcend the frontiers of modern states and occasionally become entangled in the same territory with the Melkites, Armenians, Chaldeans, Maronites, Syriacs, Copts, Malabarese, and Ethiopians.

Based on the above, the term *Orient* is not purely a politely negative word applied to non-Western churches. From Moscow to Malabar a family air unites all these churches and sets them apart.

We shall consider what has given them a complexion different from that of Roman Catholicism from the very beginning. Their evolution through the trials of the Middle Ages and of the Modern Era will help us understand all the divisions we find today, with the spiritual treasures which constitute for them their Christian past.

1. Similarly, the Reformation divided Europe, roughly speaking, into Germans and Latins.

SECTION I · FORMATION AND CONSTITUTION OF THE ORIENTAL CHURCHES

CHRISTIANITY WAS BORN in the Orient and first developed there. The Apostles founded several churches in the Orient; hence, immediately following their era, we find Christianity solidly implanted in a considerable portion of the East. In the West, on the contrary, Rome was the only church of Apostolic origin. In fact, even in the West, the Church took on an oriental appearance since it had been first developed in Eastern colonies. The cultural language of Rome until the third century was Greek.

Eastern Christendom was born, developed, and was organized independently of Rome; it was set in motion by the vigorous thrust of the Apostles and nourished by their live tradition. It had been embodied, moreover, in the midst of an old Semitic and Hellenistic culture which clearly marked its organization, its theology and its spirituality. Western Christendom, on the other hand, gradually took on a different appearance from that of Christianity in the East, and would conform to Rome in all things. Therefore, we have two different beginnings of Christianity in Oriental Catholicism and Western Catholicism, both of which are equally legitimate. Their split was merely an historical accident; they are what they are independently of this schism.

The factors which characterized and shaped Oriental Christianity are: patriarchates, theological and doctrinal struggles, liturgical families and cultural languages.

CHAPTER I · THE PATRIARCHATES

ORIGIN OF THE INSTITUTION
VARIOUS SEES

THE PATRIARCHAL INSTITUTION was the juridical and administrative framework which permitted the various aspects of Christian life in the Orient to develop as originally intended and to take root in vast autonomies. Through its efforts the Christian communities were allowed to survive during the Moslem occupation, despite their being cut off from the center of Christendom.

However, the patriarchate does not belong only to the East. Rome has the title of Patriarchate of the West, but she seldom used it apart from that of her universal primacy. Until the sixth century, the bishop of Rome acted with less authority in the West, except in Italy, than an oriental patriarch in his territory. When the ties were broken with the East, bringing about the end of papal relations with the other patriarchs, the extent of Roman patriarchal power was confused with the power of the pope as vicar of the Church. From that time on, the patriarchal character of the bishop of Rome could hardly be distinguished from his character as head of the Church. For a long time the patriarchate was practically unheard of in the West.

In the East, on the contrary, several patriarchates existed distinct from the center of primacy. The patriarchal institution in its isolated state profoundly influenced the constitution of the Oriental church.

The patriarchate is not simply an office of a dignitary set up for the benefit of administration; in a sense it belongs to the very nature of the Church. The latter is not a pure monarchy; it was founded upon Peter, and on the Twelve.

In order to be an effective body, the bishops who were spread all over the earth grouped themselves around centers. The ecclesiastical provinces[1] and the provincial synods which existed from the very first centuries in varying degrees of organization according to region permitted the bishops to form this body. The bishop of the central city was called metropolitan and his power was the nucleus of patriarchal influence.

The following four events stand out in the formation of the old patriarchates: The First Council of Nicea, the First Council of Constantinople, the Council of Chalcedon, and lastly, the Justinian Era.

Nicea. The fourth and fifth canon of the First Ecumenical Council held at Nicea in 325 defined the organization of an ecclesiastical province closely patterned after a civil province. The sixth canon recognized a supraprovincial authority in the three cities of Rome, Alexandria, and Antioch, thereby consecrating an old tradition. A parallel was set up between the powers of Rome over Italy and those of Alexandria over Egypt. In these vast regions the power of the primate was direct over the bishops, since these territories were not divided into ecclesiastical provinces.

1. Each city had its bishop. The bishops of cities belonging to the same civil province were grouped together to form an ecclesiastical province. The bishop of the capital of a province was given the title of Metropolitan in the East, and Metropolitan Archbishop in the West.

Antioch also had an honorary, but poorly defined, primacy over the seven provinces of Syria, each of which already had its own metropolitan. The preeminence of these sees stemmed from their Apostolic origin, their missionary role and from their civil importance; they were in truth the three first cities of the empire.

Constantinople. In 381 the First Council of Constantinople, which was especially concerned with the organization of the Church in the Orient, once again reflected the tendency to imitate civil administration in the episcopal grouping. The forty-nine provinces of the prefecture of the Orient were grouped into five civil dioceses.[2] Canon 2 of Constantinople discreetly superimposed this new setup, called diocese, on the ecclesiastical province. Each diocese was to be autonomous and the bishop of one was to remain independent of the bishop of another.

The Council recalled the already established privileges of Alexandria and of Antioch, the capitals of the diocese of Egypt and of the Orient, respectively. While recognizing, however, the regrouping of the other dioceses of Thra-

2. According to *Notitia Dignitatum* of 400–410 the Roman Empire was divided into four prefectures, two for the East and two for the West. Each prefecture was divided into dioceses which in turn included a given number of provinces. The Eastern Empire included the prefecture of Illyria, which included the dioceses of Dacca and Macedonia. It also included the Oriental Prefecture. From an ecclesiastical point of view Illyria answered to the Western Patriarchate until 732.

The Oriental Prefecture included the following five dioceses: Thracia with Heraclea as capital; Asia with Ephesus as capital with eleven provinces; Pontus with Caeserea as capital with eleven provinces; the Orient with Antioch as capital with fifteen provinces; and Egypt with Alexandria as capital with six provinces.

Hence the word diocese here has a much broader meaning than it has in modern usage. The diocese grouped several provinces, each of which comprised several episcopal territories, or dioceses, in today's usage.

cia, Asia, and Pontus, it did not give any special powers to
the bishops of their capitals, Heraclea, Ephesus, and
Caesarea of Cappadocia. It thus left a free hand to the
bishop of the new imperial capital, Constantinople, who
had already been divested of the jurisdiction of Heraclea,
and who had received an honorary primacy (canon 3).

Chalcedon. The Council of Chalcedon in 451 recognized the evolution which had taken place in the first half
of the fifth century. It established an exarch[3] as head of
each of the five oriental dioceses. The three provinces of
Palestine were separated from the domain of Antioch in
favor of Jerusalem which became autonomous. The ex-
archs of Heraclea, Ephesus and Caesarea were placed
under the wing of Constantinople, which took first place,
after Rome, and held a definite jurisdiction over Thracia
and Asia Minor.

Rome did not approve of canon 28 of Chalcedon, decreed in the absence of her delegates, which granted Constantinople preeminence in the East. Saint Leo protested, and the privileges of Alexandria and of Antioch
were the only ones recognized because only these sees with
Rome were of Petrine origin. Nevertheless, the organization went into full swing. The exarchates, a provisional
stage, gradually faded away until Justinian's reign.

Justinian. Justinian recognized the division of the
Church, based on the civil plan into the following five
patriarchates: Rome, Constantinople, Alexandria, Antioch,
and Jerusalem.

Rome did not enthusiastically accept this title which
joined her to the oriental system. In the Orient, a patriarchate corresponded to a firmly structured unity because

3. Exarch corresponds to primate in the West. He is the bishop of
the diocese in the old sense.

the episcopate had long since been organized into a body, whereas the ecclesiastical West lacked cohesion. Rome exercised effective patriarchal power only in Italy. Milan, however, took northern Italy at the end of the fourth century. Through his vicar in Thessalonica, the pope exercised power over eastern Illyrica including Macedonia and Greece. Illyrica was considered part of the Eastern Empire only since 379.[4] This vicar ruled over the metropolitan of Illyrica. Elsewhere in the West, in Gaul, Spain, Africa, and Britain the pope did not intervene in the ordinations of bishops or of metropolitans. He was, however, recognized as having a universal primacy of another order, which made him responsible for the faith and the discipline of the whole Church. He exercised this power directly in the West where there were no other sees or patriarchates,[5] but indirectly in the East through his associates, the patriarchs. He did intervene, however, in the East in important matters and upon request.

Though useful in the East the title of Patriarch of the West still remained ambiguous. On the one hand, it led Rome gradually to assume all of the national particularities of the West, and to become its only truly metropolitan see. On the other hand, it led the Eastern patriarchs to look upon the pope as merely the most venerable of their colleagues because the universal primacy of divine right had not been clearly defined by law.

The see of *Constantinople* owes its rank of second place

4. Once rejoined to the West, Illyrica was ceded to the eastern empire by Gratian, without ceasing to depend from an ecclesiastical point of view upon the see of Rome. This brought about frictions with Constantinople and eventually led to a show of power in 732 wherein Leo III reassigned Illyrica to the jurisdiction of Constantinople.

5. Only Milan and Carthage, and to a lesser degree Arles, were really primatial sees, but their influence rapidly vanished.

to its political prestige as capital of the empire. The eastern councils had, in fact, stipulated that the ecclesiastical boundaries would follow along the lines of civil divisions and that the religious importance of a city would grow as its civil importance grew. Canons 9 of Antioch, 34 of the Apostles, and 12 and 19 of Chalcedon bear this out. In Rome, however, these principles had no influence, and for a long time, the title of Patriarch of Constantinople was not recognized. History, however, moved on. The permanent Synod was presided over by the patriarch of Constantinople and judged the cases of bishops coming from all corners of the empire to plead their cause in the capital. It even permitted the patriarch of this city to intervene in the affairs of the patriarchs of Alexandria and Antioch. The Monophysite Schism was already weakening these two patriarchates, and this situation allowed John the Younger, Patriarch of Constantinople, to have himself called Ecumenical Patriarch in 587. Despite the protestations of Saint Gregory the Great, this title endured and the patriarch of Constantinople alone remained in the empire. The other patriarchs of the East fell during the seventh century under Arab domination. All the Oriental Christian powers now abounded in Byzantium, which became a rallying place, the center of Oriental Christianity, and the mother of Slavonic churches. Rome finally acknowledged the preeminence of Constantinople in the East. She did so implicitly, at first, in canon 21 of the Fourth Council of Constantinople in 869 and explicitly, later on, in canon 5 of the Fourth Lateran Council in 1215, and in Florence in 1439.

The patriarchate of Alexandria covered Egypt and Cyrenaica as well as Ethiopia. For a long time the Egyptian patriarch remained the only metropolitan. He ordained all of the bishops of Egypt, whose churches were under his wing. For this reason he was compared to a pharaoh.

The patriarchate of Antioch from which Persia in 424, Cyprus in 431 and Jerusalem in 451 were separated, comprised twelve provinces made up of 153 episcopates in the sixth century. It encompassed the South of Asia Minor, namely Isauria and Cilicia, Syria as far as the Taurus mountains and spread its influence into Georgia. It was the junction of Semitic and Hellenistic cultures.

These two patriarchates of Alexandria and Antioch were the most highly regarded in the East because of their antiquity, and their theological, liturgical, and missionary roles.

The patriarchate of Jerusalem included three provinces and forty-eight bishoprics. The Holy City had been assigned a place of honor by Nicea, but remained a simple bishopric, dependent on Caesarea of Palestine, which was a metropolitan see deriving its power from Antioch. Its bishops succeeded in disengaging themselves from Caesarea in the fourth century. At the Council of 451, the ambitious Juvenal obtained his autonomy and extended the jurisdiction of the Holy City to include the three provinces of Palestine. This patriarchate preserved a strong affinity towards Antioch in its liturgy and cultural languages. Because of the ceremonies of the Holy Land and the many pilgrimages there, its influence on the rest of Christendom was tremendous; its liturgical customs were introduced into nearly every Church.[6]

6. Why did Jerusalem rank only fifth and why so late? It seems to me that this is due to the destruction of Jerusalem in the year 70. The new community of Jerusalem was thus cut off from the old. Moreover, the mother-community of Jerusalem had been a focal point among the Jews. Antioch was the focal point for the pagans until the fourth century. The focus on Antioch was the most wide-

THE NATURE OF A PATRIARCHATE

The patriarchal reality is not made up solely of the dignity and the power of the patriarch. The patriarchate as territory is an established, homogeneous unity, which enjoys a broad autonomy. It corresponds to a human, sociopolitical reality. The powers of the patriarch are developed more or less according to the patriarchate, where he not only holds a primacy of honor, but an effective primacy of jurisdiction as well. He fills vacant sees and consecrates metropolitans; he makes final decisions throughout the patriarchate and enjoys the rights of allegiance and of inspection. The law reserves for him the preparation of the holy oils which he personally distributes to the bishops. His name is mentioned in the sacred liturgy with the name of the local bishop. Emperors, and especially califs and sultans, have granted far-reaching civil prerogatives to him.

THE PENTARCHY

The patriarchs were not only responsible for their respective territories in the East, but were also deeply involved in the direction of the whole Church. The five patriarchs, with the patriarch of Rome having preeminence, formed a college known as the Pentarchy which headed the Church. The Byzantine canonists greatly elaborated on this point. Rome did not readily accept the Pentarchy, being reluctant to recognize the recent prerogatives of Constantinople and of Jerusalem, but she did admit to

---

spread in Christendom. After the year 70, moreover, Jerusalem's reduced political importance also contributed to the lessening of its ecclesiastical rank.

a sort of Triarchy, or a direction by three. Pope Saint Gregory wrote to the patriarchs of Antioch and of Alexandria as to his colleagues as follows: "Saint Peter, who founded these sees, continues to occupy them in the persons who succeed him in each of these sees."

Rome, however, retained her preeminence and primary responsibility in the Church. The patriarchs were required to remain in communion with her and to conform to her faith. She intervened in the East by right of appeal to her supreme tribunal or whenever a matter of faith was in question.

The relations among the five patriarchs maintained unity and cohesion in the Church. Each patriarch-elect would send a synodal letter to his colleagues announcing his election and containing his profession of faith; their reply, in turn, was their way of confirming their recognition. In the sacred liturgy, each patriarch mentioned the others at the Commemoration of the Living in the diptychs. We also note that each one had personal representatives which were called *apocrisarii*.

THE CATHOLICOSATES

Outside the Roman Empire, the principle of the pentarchy was already disrupted by the establishment of two ecclesiastical autonomies, whose leaders gave themselves the title of *catholicos*. These were the churches of Persia and Armenia.

Christianity came into Persia very early in the first century, probably through Edessa. It developed especially in the Arbela region, and in Mesopotamia, in the Semitic regions where Aramaic was spoken, and where the numerous Jews from Babylonia were receptive to Christianity.

The bishop of Seleucia-Ctesiphon, the imperial capital, succeeded in gathering around him all of the episcopal sees of the Persian Empire, while maintaining his dependence on Antioch and the Western Fathers.[7] The church of Antioch at the Synod of 410 helped the Persian church to reorganize itself after the countless persecutions it suffered at the hands of the ever-pagan Persian emperors. To accomplish this, it took advantage of the rest periods during an almost continuous war between the two rival empires of Rome and Persia. The tension, however, remained constant and the Christians were always suspected of compromising with the Roman enemy because of their common faith. As a result the relations between the two churches gradually deteriorated. It was not until the year 410 that the church of Persia officially accepted the decisions of the Council of Nicea in 325.

Although 424 is generally given as the date of the split with Antioch, this date appears to be doubtful, because the Acts of the Synod of 424 seem to be apocryphal. In fact, the relations between the two churches were of very short duration and ended towards the end of the fifth century owing to the particular doctrinal switch relative to Christology taken by the Persian Church. This church of Persia presented the oddity of being a church which from its start was cut off from Hellenism. It was, moreover, in the Jewish biblical line and was not influenced by Greek philosophy. In addition, it had never been under any Christian political regime.

Christianity came into Armenia through the missionaries of Syria and Caesarea of Cappadocia. Saint Gregory the Illuminator at the beginning of the fourth century converted the king and organized the church. He had been

7. To the Persians, Syrians were westerners.

consecrated bishop by the bishop of Caesarea and for that reason set up his church in this metropolis. In 374 this church declared itself independent and clearly assumed the aspect of a national church.

Armenia, the apple of discord between Rome and Persia, was partitioned in the year 387. The Emperor Theodosius obtained one-fifth of the territory which he promptly joined to the Roman Empire. The remainder went into the Persian domain. After a period of semi-freedom, the last of the Armenian sovereigns, Arsacidan, died in 428, and there were no more successors. From that time on, the church assumed the national conscience and later its first see was to change its title.

The catholicoses of Persia and Armenia were both assimilated as inferiors by the patriarchs and their delegates. In Persia, however, the catholicos gave himself the title of patriarch sometime in the sixth century.

We must also mention here that there were two churches outside the empire, in Georgia and in Ethiopia, which had definite personalities of their own, but which did not secede as had Persia and Armenia. For a long time Georgia remained dependent on Antioch. Ethiopia obtained its autonomy from the Coptic patriarch of Alexandria only in 1959; her primate received the title of patriarch-catholicos to designate his dependence upon Alexandria.

THE NEW PATRIARCHATES

As time went on, the principle of pentarchy was to take on new turns. Without disclosing their internal schisms to the patriarchs of Alexandria and Antioch, the new nationalities, which sprang up in the East during the Middle

Ages and the Modern Era, were inclined to set up autonomous patriarchates such as those in Bulgaria, Serbia,
Russia, and Rumania.

The catholicosates and these new patriarchates had a real
significance inasmuch as they centralized the religious in-
terests of a nation and leaned on a socio-political unity.
But they were only primates and their authority was to
disappear or to be modified with the disappearance of their
independence or with the change of frontiers. Even their
title would disappear entirely, which is why they are
known as the minor patriarchates.

Such was not the case with the ancient or major patriarchates, like those of Alexandria and Antioch, which were
especially important. As we have seen, their authority was
recognized by the Council of Nicea and their primacy
was considered to be of apostolic right; the popes of the
first centuries looked upon this primacy as a participation in
the authority of Peter, founder of these sees. We note too
that their importance in Christendom was not diminished
by any reduction in the number of their dependents. They
were more than branch offices or directors of Roman
bureaus.

We must not group the patriarchates of the East with
the purely honorary patriarchates found in the Western
Church, such as the patriarchates of Venice, Lisbon, Goa,
or the Latin patriarchate of Jerusalem.

On the other hand, nothing prevents Rome from establishing true patriarchates in China, India, or in black
Africa, since these countries can be considered as part of
the Western patriarchate. During the Crusades, the Latins
established Franks as patriarchs, with far-reaching powers
over the eastern sees; during the Middle Ages, the primatial see of Canterbury received the pallium from

Rome and enjoyed considerable autonomy with some important delegated powers. Based on the above, we see that all patriarchs were not meant to be placed on the same level. Thus we distinguish major patriarchates of apostolic right, minor patriarchates assimilated by primates, and honorary patriarchates.

CHAPTER II · THEOLOGICAL LIFE AND DOCTRINAL STRUGGLES

THEOLOGICAL LIFE

THE ORIENT of old was passionately interested in theology. Christians, however, formed in Hellenism and imbued with Stoic, Neo-Platonic or Aristotelian philosophy, did not always give up their taste for speculation. Along with a traditional current, rooted in the exposition of faith in biblical terms, a speculative current came to life which borrowed its language from philosophy. This was a dangerous road which led many writers away from the traditional faith, such as the heretics, and led others to attempt to express the true faith in philosophical concepts. Although their formulas were not always happy choices, little by little they helped to prepare dogmatic definitions.

From the second century on, Rome was invaded by oriental Christians who came to teach her their doctrines. Both heretics and orthodox mingled as, for example, St. Justin, Tatian, Marcion, and Valentine. In the third century this current diminished, because well-organized schools were established and supported by the hierarchy. Among these, the best known were the schools of Alexandria and Antioch. These displayed clearly opposed tendencies.

The School of Alexandria, established at the end of the second century by Pantemus, blossomed during the third century with Clement, Origen, and Denys, Bishop of Alexandria. The new school of the fourth century gained prominence, with such great writers as St. Athanasius, Didymus, and St. Cyril. With a Neo-Platonic penchant, these writers stressed the mysterious and the transcendental; in exegesis, they preferred the mystical and allegorical interpretation. They insisted on the divinity of Christ and his substantial unity. Despite the errors in language regarding the dogma of the Trinity before the Council of Nicea, their sense of tradition and mystery kept them within orthodoxy. However, because of their poorly enlightened and excessively literal attachment to tradition and to St. Cyril's formulas, Egypt slumbered into Monophysitism.

The School of Antioch was more positive; it followed St. Lucian of Antioch, disciple of Paul of Samosata. Its most illustrious representatives in the fourth and fifth centuries were Flavian, Diodorus of Tarsus, Theodore of Mopsuestia, St. John Chrysostom, and Theodoret of Cyrrhus. Leaning more towards Aristotelianism, they accentuated the human and the rational; in exegesis, they favored the literal and historical meaning, because of their moralistic rather than mystical tendencies. In trinitarian theology they accentuated the distinction of persons; in Christology they insisted on the human reality of Christ and the duality of the human and the divine, and left somewhat in the dark the question of substantial unity. Some theologians, too confident in the rational methods of their school and allowing themselves a slightly bolder free-

dom with regard to tradition, led the thinking towards the
Arian and Nestorian errors. Although collaboration between these schools sought to be a way to truth, their
opposition was to provoke serious religious quarrels during
the fourth and fifth centuries.

DOCTRINAL CONTROVERSIES

Unfortunately these doctrinal controversies were not
limited to a group of specialists. The school tendencies,
mixing with the rivalries of the large sees, with personal
quarrels, and a rising national sentiment, enflamed the
passions of mobs, excited monks, and led emperors to intervene in church affairs. All of this was not conducive to
serene study or to a fraternal dialogue relative to these delicate questions.

We cannot go into the complete history of these controversies here because it is too complex and calls into play
too many subtle notions. Let us try merely to extract their
object, the broad outline of their evolution, and their effects on the life of the Church.

The object of these doctrinal struggles was revealed by
the oriental spirit from the beginning. Although the Christian West also was passionately interested in theology ever
since antiquity, it was from a more practical or disciplinary
point of view and with the emphasis on man. Philosophy
came into play only with St. Augustine. It was the peni-
tential discipline, an attitude of taking to task the re-
pentent apostates, which occasioned the Novatian Schism
and that of the Donatists. It also called into question the
validity of Baptism performed by heretics. In the same
manner the questions of freedom, and sin, of nature, and
grace, gave rise to the Pelagian controversy.

The Orient was deeply concerned with the central mystery of Christianity manifested by the Word made flesh, at once God and man. The intellectual contemplation of this mystery was the source of its conceptual expression. It faced the following problems:

———How to express the relationship of Christ with the Father, in such a way as to safeguard his distinction from the Father, as well as his divinity and the divine unity of the Creator?

———How to express the relationship of the Christ-God with human nature, in such a way as to safeguard the reality of his divine nature, as well as his human nature and the unity of his existential being?

The first question posed the trinitarian problem debated in the third, and especially in the fourth century; the second, the christological problem, was to be the object of study in the fifth and sixth centuries. Let us briefly examine each one.

THE TRINITARIAN CONTROVERSY

Until the end of the third century we did not have an adequate expression of the Blessed Trinity. Some insisted so much on the divine unity and the equality of Persons, that they no longer saw in them distinct Persons. Such was the Modalist danger. Others, teaching the reality and distinction of Three Persons, did not succeed in safeguarding the divine unity, except by subordination of the Son and the Spirit to the Father. This was Subordinationism. The first of these tendencies was strong in the West, the second in the East.

At the beginning of the fourth century, Arius, a priest of Alexandria, but trained at Antioch and a disciple of Lucian, professed a clear Subordinationism as follows: The Word was brought forth from nothing by the Father. The Word was a likeness to the substance of the Father, a secondary God, creator of all things, even of the Holy Spirit. Arius was supported by his fellow students at Antioch, but was condemned by his bishop, Alexander, who saw fit to take a stand when the conflict spread. In 325 at the request of Constantine the entire episcopate met for the first time at Nicea, and Arius was officially condemned. They adopted the formula of faith, since known as the Nicene Creed: "We believe in only One God, Father Almighty, and in only One Lord Jesus Christ, Son of God, True God of True God, begotten, not made, consubstantial with the Father."

The Greek term *homoousios*, corresponding to consubstantial, had not been readily accepted by all the orientals. It had been disapproved by the Council of Antioch in 268, because Paul of Samosata, who was being judged by that Council, used this term in a modalistic sense, denying the distinction of Persons. The opposition at the Council was not led by Arius, but by Eusebius of Nicomedia, also a student of Lucian of Antioch. The most ardent champion of the Nicene faith, on the other hand, was Athanasius. Having been circumvented by Eusebius, Constantine exiled the principal Orthodox bishops who were replaced by Arianists. A half century of religious battles was required to bring about the triumph of the Nicene faith. At one time, in 359 under Emperor Constans, Arianism almost won out. The flexibility of the Three Cappadocian Fathers, St. Basil, St. Gregory of Nazianzus and St. Gregory of Nyssa, who were better dialectitians than Athanasius, carried the support of the semi-Arians.[1] They had accepted as counterpart to *homoousios* the formula of three hypostases,[2] which was repugnant to Athanasius.

The Council held in Constantinople in 381 under Emperor Theodosius formulated a more complete doctrine on the Word and defined the divinity of the Holy Spirit. Although Orthodoxy triumphed in the empire, a certain misunderstanding impregnated the Rome-Antioch relations until 398, the date of reconciliation.[3] Outside the

1. The anti-Nicene doctrine was subject to variations. Besides the intransigent Arians or Anonians, according to whom the Son of God is different from the Father, there were the Homoians who held that the Son of God simply resembles the Father, and the group of moderate semi-Arians or, Homoousians, for whom the Son resembles the Father in substance. One iota separated them from the Nicean ὁμοιουσιος instead of ὁμοουσιος. For this iota, Athanasius and Basil accepted the persecutions of Emperor Valens.

2. The word ὑπόστασις corresponds literally to substance. It was synonymous to οὐσία (essence for the westerners and the Alexandrians. The latter were reluctant to admit three hypostases in God. They preferred to speak of three persons, in Greek: προσωπον, but this term, borrowed, from the theatre signified role or mask. For the Antiochians, it gave rise to Modalism. This is why the school of Antioch spoke of three hypostases to designate the ontological consistency of the three. It distinguished, however, the hypostasis from the "οὐσία." The Cappadocians accepted their terminology.

3. It was the famous schism of Antioch. Apart from the Arians who occupied the episcopal see from 336–360, there were the moderate Orthodox and the intransigents. The moderates recognized Meletius as the duly elected bishop who frankly declared his orthodoxy. The Arians, on the other hand, supported an opposing bishop. The intransigents did not want to recognize him, and succeeded in having their chief, Paulinus, a priest, consecrated bishop. This was an irregularity which became more complicated when Rome recognized Paulinus. The Orient, with St. Basil, favored Meletius. As it happened, the latter opened the Council of Constantinople. The followers of Paulinus also gave him a successor. Finally Rome had the wisdom to drop him and recognize Flavian in 398 at the request of John Chrysostom, his disciple. The opposition dragged on until the middle of the fifth century.

empire, the Goths in southern Russia preserved the Arianism they had received from their evangelizers. By spreading into Western Europe, they were to bring back religious division into certain regions for two or three centuries.

THE CHRISTOLOGICAL CONTROVERSY

Christ appears in the Scriptures simultaneously as God and man. Even as God, He is distinct from the Father and the Holy Spirit. This is how we have come to know the mystery of the Blessed Trinity, but, having admitted this mystery, the christological problem, so-called, remains in its entirety. How is Christ at once God and man, while he is a being existentially One? What is the relationship of the human to the divine in Christ? The Antiochians insisted on the subsistence of the two elements, divine and human, thus making their unity arduously intelligible. The Alexandrians stressed the unity of the divine being in Christ, but insufficiently explained the subsistence in him of the divine and the human. The former rightly affirmed that Christ possesses two complete natures, but considered the union of the two natures as purely moral, since, for Aristotle, the union of two complete substances was accidental. The latter, wanting to safeguard the unity of Christ, admitted that "he is of two natures" but refused to maintain that "he is in two natures." The confrontation of these two tendencies provoked long controversies which, with the efforts made to arrive at a synthesis at Chalcedon, led to the development of dogma.

Apollinarianism. The controversies which were very much heated in the fifth and sixth centuries had already been under way at the end of the fourth century; at that time, however, no attention was paid to them because interest was focused on the Nicene dogma.

Apollinaris, Bishop of Laodicea in Syria (390), an ardent defender of Nicea, in order to establish solidly the divinity of Christ, denied the reality of his human nature. He maintained that the Word had taken on a human body, and that the role of an intelligent soul had been assured by the Word. Denounced by St. Basil, he was condemned in 377 by Pope St. Damasus, a condemnation which was to be taken up again by several oriental councils. The writings of Apollinaris were spread by his disciples under well-known pseudonyms, such as St. Jules, and St. Athanasius. St. Cyril, too, allowed himself to be swayed, and borrowed from Apollinaris the formula: "unique is the nature of the Word of God Incarnate."

Nestorianism. The masters of the School of Antioch were the most ardent opponents of Apollinaris; they insisted on the reality of the human nature of Christ and the duality of his Being. Diodore of Tarsus (392) distinguished two Sons in Christ; "the Son of God," he wrote, "took the Son of David and lived in him; the man born of Mary is not the Son of God by nature." He was thus the precursor of the theory of the double personality and moral union, which was to be developed by his disciple, Theodore of Mopsuestia (428), who maintained that the union of the Word with man is not a substantial union, but a friendly one. At that moment, Theodore denied, against all tradition, the *communicatio idiomatum* which enables one to say that God died or that Mary is the Mother of God. While Diodore and Theodore escaped censure during their lifetime, Nestorius, whose doctrine was somewhat more nuanced than that of his master, Theodore, drew the disputations of St. Cyril. He was condemned, and the error still bears his name. Priest and monk of Antioch, he became bishop of Constantinople in 428. From the very start he was a strong fighter against heresies, and wanted to avoid the use of the title *Theotokos,* or Mother of God. Pope Celestine condemned him and demanded that he adhere to the formula of Rome and of Alexandria, and instructed St. Cyril, Bishop of Alexandria, to carry out the sentence. The latter sent twelve christological formulas to Nestorius which he requested him to sign; but, in the eyes of Nestorius and the Antiochians, these formulations of anathemas, due to their terminology, were Apollinaristic. The bishop of Constantinople replied to his colleague from Alexandria with twelve counteranathemas.

Meanwhile, at Nestorius' request, an ecumenical council was held at Ephesus in 431. St. Cyril directed this council which was to condemn Nestorius, define the divine maternity of Mary and adopt the christological formulas presented by St. Cyril. Nestorius agreed to retire in a monastery; John, Bishop of Antioch, and his suffragan did not adhere to the decisions of the council, which had been made before their arrival, and St. Cyril was excommunicated.

In 433 at the request of both pope and emperor, John of Antioch and Cyril of Alexandria were reconciled. To avoid a schism, Cyril made some concessions; he gave up the formulas unique nature and physical union. The Orientals, on the other hand, recognized the condemnation of Nestorius and accepted the title of *Theotokos* as well as the *communicatio idiomatum.* This reconciliation so-called displeased the intransigents on both sides. Among the friends of St. Cyril, there were some real Monophysites;

and, in the East, many remained loyal to Nestorius.[4] The theses of Nestorius having been condemned, his followers spread the writings of Theodore of Mopsuestia, and translated them into Syriac and Armenian. Proclus, Bishop of Constantinople, who had been consulted in this matter, put the Armenians on guard in a work often referred to as the *Tome of St. Proclus* and insisted on the unity of Christ, thereby drawing the Armenians toward Monophysitism.

On the other hand, Nestorianism triumphed among the Persians; Edessa, next door, was the main distribution center for Theodore's writings, thanks to Ibas of Edessa. Pressed by the Monophysite emperors, many professors from the School of Edessa went to Nisibis and reorganized their school.[5] As a result, the Antiocheans' dualism spread in this empire and soon became the official doctrine of the church of Persia, which, from that time on, was known as "The Nestorian church,"[6] and recognized Theodore of Mopsuestia as a great Doctor of the Church (Synods of 484, 486). But its Nestorianism, under the leadership of its most influential Doctor, Catholicos Babai (627), began to weaken in a Catholic sense.

Monophysitism. The anti-Nestorian formulas of St. Cyril could be understood in a Monophysite sense, which excludes the permanence of the two natures after the union. Eutyches, Abbot of Constantinople, interpreted them by denying that Christ was consubstantial with us.

4. Theodoret of Cyrrhus was sullen toward his archbishop, John, for a long time.

5. The most active was Barsumas who became Bishop of Nisibis.

6. At that time, Monophysitism was in vogue in the Byzantine Empire; these Christians of Persia thereby displayed again their broken ties with their rivals. At the instigation of Barsumas, the pagan emperor, Peroz, recognized Nestorianism as the official doctrine and proscribed the other christological doctrines.

Having been condemned by a synod held at Constantinople in 448, he appealed to Pope St. Leo, who confirmed the condemnation; but the Monk received the support of Emperor Theodosius II and of Dioscorus who succeeded St. Cyril in the see of Alexandria in 444.

At an irregular council, known as the Robber Council of Ephesus held at Ephesus in the year 449, Dioscorus reinstated Eutyches while Theodoret of Cyrrhus and Ibas of Edessa were condemned; the delegates were not permitted to read the dogmatic Tome sent by St. Leo, who strongly protested to no avail. Emperor Theodosius II died while this was going on. In 451 Marcian, his successor, ordered the convocation of a general council at Nicea, a council which was moved to Chalcedon and afterwards known under this name.[7] Dioscorus was deposed; Theodoret and Ibas were reinstated after agreeing to anathematize Nestorius. Finally, the doctrine presented in the Tome of St. Leo was adopted, despite a small group which did not want new definitions. St. Leo defined the unity of the Son in two natures, without any change in either of the natures, each keeping its own properties and uniting itself in a single Person, or hypostasis, not in two Persons.

The formula of St. Cyril, *of two natures*, gave way to that of St. Leo, *in two natures*. The bishops' acceptance of this, however, was not enthusiastic, and many considered returning to Nestorianism. Up to that time in Alexandria as well as in Antioch the terms nature and hypostasis were used interchangeably. Chalcedon, with its Western formula, did not succeed in bringing religious peace to the Orient; it met with tenacious opposition, first in Egypt and Palestine, where veritable armed conflicts

7. More than five hundred bishops were counted, all oriental except for the four papal delegates and two Africans.

were waged; then in Syria, where the most solid theologians of Monophysitism were found, such as Philoxenus of Mabbug and Severus of Antioch. A century-long crisis was to plunge these countries into an irreparable schism. We shall follow only the broad outlines of this painful struggle which preoccupied the emperors as much as the pressure of the barbarians had done.

Marcian, who died in 457, gave his complete support to the council, and intervened militarily in Egypt and Palestine. When he died, the mob revolted in Alexandria and massacred Proterius, the Catholic Bishop, who had replaced the deposed Dioscorus. Leo, the new Emperor, (457–474) chastised the guilty ones, but for a little while kept Timothy Aelurus, the choice of the Monophysites; calm was restored in Palestine, thanks to the efforts of St. Euthymius and his disciples. In the patriarchate of Antioch, the Monophysite opposition settled down in the Mesopotamian section, as Peter Fullo, of Monophysite leanings, succeeded in occupying the patriarchal throne on several separate occasions.

Under the Emperors Zeno (474–491) and Anastasius (491–518) the imperial political view favored Monophysitism. Zeno allowed the exiled Monophysite bishop to return; at the instigation of Acacius, Patriarch of Constantinople, he promulgated an Edict of Unity in 482, called the *Henoticon* which imposed the decisions of the first three councils, condemned Nestorius and Eutyches, made no mention of Chalcedon, the Fourth Council, but condemned everything outside of the first three councils. Most of the titulars of the oriental sees signed the *Henoticon*, but Pope Felix III condemned it and broke off with Acasius.

At first, Anastasius hid his Monophysite feelings; peace

returned and many Monophysites adhered to Chalcedon. However, in the year 506, the battle was rekindled by Philoxenus, Bishop of Mabbug on the Euphrates and Severus, who replaced the Chalcedonian bishop of Antioch from 512 to 518. Severus was the great theologian of modified Monophysitism who condemned both Eutyches and Nestorius, but adhered to the christology and formulas of St. Cyril, without recognizing the dogmatic progress of Chalcedon.

Justin, the Emperor (518–527), reacted against Monophysitism and solemnly reestablished Orthodoxy, except in Egypt where Severus of Antioch later went to find refuge.

Justinian (527–565) was Orthodox, but his wife, Theodora, was Monophysite. With the hope of bringing back the Monophysites to the faith of Chalcedon, he organized several theological religious conferences in Constantinople, where he agreed to many compromises.[8] The arrival of Pope Agapetus in Constantinople in 536 gave rise to a strong reaction in favor of Orthodoxy, and the Orthodox hierarchy was reestablished even in Egypt. Thanks to Theodora, however, the deposed patriarch of Alexandria, Theodosius, was brought to Constantinople where he secretly consecrated numerous bishops. In 543, at the request of the Ghassanid prince, Al Harith, then in conflict with Justinian, Theodosius consecrated Jacob Baradai, Bishop of Ephesus and Ecumenical Metropolitan. In a

8. The chief Chalcedonian theologian was Leontius of Byzantium (542), who attempted to point out the agreement between the different conciliar definitions. He established particularly the distinction between nature and hypostasis. A nature can be real without being hypostasis, being simply inherent in the hypostasis, *"enhypostaton"*; after him the theology of the hypostatic union would not make much progress.

most extraordinary move, Jacob went all over the Orient, consecrating bishops and setting them up beside the existing Orthodox hierarchy. Hence, the constitution of the Monophysite churches can be traced back to this date 543;[9] in the last half of the sixth century they were able to organize themselves, thanks to the tolerance of Justinian's successors, Tiberius and Maurice. These churches embodied the national opposition to the empire. The Monophysite church of the patriarchate of Antioch became the Syrian-Jacobite church, named after James or Jacob Baradai, which is made up mainly of the regions of Syriac culture. The Monophysite church of the patriarchate of Alexandria became the Coptic church, that is Egyptian, which meant that henceforth Coptic would be its official language. Ethiopia was to follow the Egyptian majority in opposition to Chalcedon; in Palestine, though, Monophysitism did not take root, thanks to the zeal of St. Sabas and the influence of his monastery.

The Chalcedonian partisans in the three patriarchates of Alexandria, Antioch and Jerusalem were surnamed Melkites or Royalists by their adversaries, because their Orthodoxy was looked upon as a slavish adherence to the dictates of the emperor. Armenia, under Persian domination, could not participate in all these events; favoring Monophysitism, thanks to the spread of the *Tome of St. Proclus,* she was somehow absent from the Council of Chalcedon and because of the Persian persecution did not take part in the discussions which preceded and followed it. When she was able to reestablish relations with Rome, it was in the era of the *Henoticon.* The Armenians condemned Chalcedon in 491 at the Council of Vagarchapat

9. Before this date the Monophysites did not form a distinct church.

and avoided the reinstating of Justinian. The Armenian church thus became Monophysite and, in 526, excommunicated those of the Byzantine church; her neighbor, Georgia, accepted Chalcedon and thus manifested her independence from Armenia.

Hence, at the end of the sixth century, only the patriarchates of Constantinople and Jerusalem remained completely Orthodox; the Persian church was Nestorian, the Armenian church Monophysite. The patriarchates of Alexandria and Antioch were each split up into the Monophysite branch and the Orthodox-Melkite branch. Later there was to be a third branch in Antioch, namely, the Maronite patriarchate, resulting from the Monothelite quarrel of the seventh century.

Monothelitism. Right to the end of his reign, Justinian dreamed of reconciling the Monophysites; this is why he pressed the Second Council of Constantinople in 553, the Fifth Ecumenical Council, to condemn the writings of authors suspected of Nestorianism, even those who had been reinstated at the Council of Chalcedon.[10] This effort was to no avail, because, after the death of the Emperor, the Monophysites organized themselves and became a grave threat to the unity of the Empire.

At the beginning of the seventh century Sergius, Patriarch of Constantinople, in an effort to rally the Monophysites, toned down the Chalcedonian doctrine and

10. These writings are known as *The Three Chapters.*
They are: 1. The writings of Theodore of Mopsuestia.
2. The letter of Ibas of Edessa to the Persian, Maris.
3. Theodoret of Cyrrhus' defense of Nestorius against St. Cyril and the Council of Ephesus.

The Council attacked Theodore of Mopsuestia and merely studied superficially the writings of the other two authors.

defined a more moderate one which he hoped would be acceptable to all churches. He maintained that we should recognize two natures in Christ, but only one theandric operation and one will, thus Monothelitism. This meant emptying the human nature of all consistency and reducing it to a purely passive instrument, which was closer to Apollinarianism and Monophysitism than to Chalcedon.

Instead of achieving the desired union, these concessions, which were forceably imposed by Emperors Heraclitus and Constans II, gave rise to religious battles for a half century. St. Sophronius of Jerusalem and St. Maximus Confessor were the great adversaries of Monothelitism, which was finally condemned in 681 by the Third Council of Constantinople, the sixth ecumenical council, which recognized in Christ two natural operations and two physical wills.

The Maronite autonomy can be traced to this troubled period when, at some unspecified date, John Maro, a monk from the monastery located between Apamea and Emesa on the Orontes River, was proclaimed Patriarch of Antioch by a group of partisans. The Maronites, or disciples of John Maro, escaped to Lebanon and joined the Lebanese opposition to Syria which was integrated with the Arabian, then Turkish Empire. Before the twelfth century, however, little is mentioned about them. Their church maintained no relation, either with the Orthodox churches of the Orient or with Rome. The Maronites of today, in order to defend their Catholic loyalty, say that their church always adhered to the true faith; but William of Tyre, the historian of the Crusades, speaks of their conversion to Monothelitism in 1182. Even long before him, the Melkite authors, such as John Damascene, Abuqurra, Eutychius of Alexandria, during the eighth to the tenth centuries, treated Maronites and Monothelites as one and the same group. The Jacobite Bishop, Abou Raita in the ninth century distinguishes two Melkite branches: the Maronites and the Maximianites, partisans of St. Maximus, the adversary of Monothelitism. Whatever the case may be, the Maronites who deserved so much from Catholicism seem to have been excellent Melkites from the beginning; however, once isolated on their mountain to resist the Arab conquest, undoubtedly in good faith, they did not ratify the official condemnation of Monothelitism at the sixth council.

BALANCE SHEET OF THE STRUGGLES

The Orient alone was the battleground of the dogmas of the Trinity and the Incarnation which we peacefully possess today; the West only intervened by way of Roman authority. The Oriental church was to come out of these battles considerably weakened and torn. This situation has persisted even to our day. When Arabia opened up in the sixth century, it was faced with a divided, Syrian Christianity, incapable of responding to its religious aspirations, yet Arabia was ready to give herself to anyone who spoke to her of God.

The patriarchates of Alexandria and Antioch were to lose their leading role in the liturgical, theological and ecclesiastical life of the Church. Constantinople alone was destined to hold this role, with Rome; she was to embody Oriental Orthodoxy.

The Orthodox Orient was to be known, in its inner life, for its true faith based on the first councils. The trinitarian doxologies, the invocations to Christ-God and to the Theotokos, the trinitarian and christological formulas

which form the basis of the liturgy and the Divine Office,
testify to past struggles. They are today a public expression
of faith, and at the same time, a dogmatic catechism directed to all the faithful.

CHAPTER III · THE LITURGICAL FAMILIES

PLACE AND CHARACTER OF LITURGY
IN THE ORIENT

ONE OF THE characteristic marks of the Christian Orient is the central place which the liturgy occupies in her church life. The contemplative East feels a calling to adoration and homage of the Infinite, a calling to ritual and to solemn celebration of the central mystery of salvation. On the other hand, the liturgy has remained close to the people; it has nourished their piety and enlightened their faith as their church reflected the spirit proper to each civilization and culture.

Liturgy in the Orient is part of the cultural patrimony of a nation;[1] it is not, as has been understood for too long in the West, a ceremonial of interest principally to clerics. Western priests who adopt the oriental liturgy feel strange if they have not assimilated oriental culture, if they have not converted their souls into an oriental one. To adopt the oriental rite does not mean simply to change Missal or Breviary. Liturgy is not a purely arbitrary ceremonial;

1. This explains the oriental's attachment to his liturgy and his defiance of the efforts of Latinists in the Orient.

41

it only makes sense as an expression of the whole cultural and ecclesiastical community which transmits to it its faith and contemplative piety in an artistic ritual language consistent with its genius.

Over and above the importance given to the liturgical celebration and to an oriental's attachment to his rite, what strikes the average westerner is the diversity of oriental liturgies.[2] This should not come as a complete surprise, since liturgies are not formed by a decree; they have required a long time to establish and organize themselves, in an atmosphere of freedom as it existed in each local church. Only the themes to be developed and the general program were common to all, conforming, so it seems, to the practice of the first community of Jerusalem. But some forms of celebration and some formulas of prayers were repeated, became customs, and later became law. The small towns patterned themselves after the practice of the large ecclesiastical metropolis, which gradually imposed itself and became more uniform within the widespread circumscriptions corresponding to the sociocultural or national unities. In fact, "Every considerable culture," writes Rev. P. Dalmais, "is invited to expand and excel itself in a liturgy, in institutions and ways of Christian living, that are particular expressions of the common faith."[3]

In the West during the Middle Ages the Roman rite was not the only one practiced; there was, particularly in France, the Gallican rite, more live and closer to the Orient. All particularities which did not have the support of an autonomous ecclesiastical organization, or a suf-

2. Many westerners do not even suspect that celebration of the Mass is possible other than in the Roman rite. Very rare are those who know of the existence of several living oriental liturgies.

3. Irenée Henri Dalmais, *Eastern Liturgies,* trans. Donald Attwater (New York: Hawthorn Books, 1960), p. 34.

ficiently original culture, were absorbed in the West by Roman centralization. Some very localized particularities persisted, like those of the Ambrosian and the Lyons rites, not to mention the Mozarabic rite found in a chapel of Toledo.

The Orient, with its various patriarchates, was preserved from a similar uniformity. Besides the Byzantine rite, which is the most widespread and best known in the West, we actually distinguish the Armenian, the Coptic, the Syriac, the Maronite and the Chaldean rites. Each of these rites is a complete liturgical system, made up of proper formularies for the celebration of the Eucharist, of the sacraments and sacramentals, and of the Divine Office. Each has its particular calendar, and its own sacred art including the architecture of churches, form of liturgical vestments, sacred chant, etc. They have some points in common, and are more or less directly based on the old rites of Antioch and Alexandria; in fact, we can recognize among them traces of interrelation which permit us to place them into two liturgical families, namely, the Syrian and the Alexandrian.

THE SYRIAN LITURGICAL FAMILY

The primitive liturgy of Antioch is the most clearly documented in antiquity; and specialists have been able to reconstruct its history from the third and fourth centuries.[4]

---

4. The principal documents are: *The Didascalia of the Apostles,* an anonymous ecclesiastical document of the middle of the third century; *The Apostolic Constitutions,* a correction of the preceding work, dating from the end of the fourth century; *The Mystagogic Catecheses* preached at Antioch by Theodore of Mopsuestia and John Chrysostom, and at Jerusalem by St. Cyril, bishop of the Holy City; *The Report of the Pilgrimage of Etheria. The Apostolic Tradition,* canonical and

The Antiochian anaphora underlines the economy of salvation, the eschatological expectation and the splendor of divine glory; it is a characteristic which has remained in the Syrian rite.

Outside of Antioch, there are two other liturgical families at Edessa and Jerusalem. The customs of Jerusalem fused rapidly with those of Antioch, while those of Edessa spread through Mesopotamia and Persia. The Chaldean rite came into being by borrowing elements from Antioch and from some developments born in the Nestorian church of Persia from the seventh to the twelfth centuries. Such is the eastern branch of the Syrian liturgical family.

The customs of Antioch which developed in the Jacobite branch of the patriarchate, with some adaptations of the liturgy of Jerusalem and Constantinople, formed the Syriac or pure Antiochian rite. The particular evolution of the Maronite branch which escaped to Lebanon, became the Maronite rite. These two rites make up the Western branch of the Syrian liturgical family.

The Byzantine rite came from the customs of Antioch and their developments in the Melkite church, during the sixth to the eighth centuries. These spread to Constantinople where they were modified by customs borrowed from the Asians who came from Caesarea of Cappadocia. Similarly, the Armenian rite resulted from a convergence of the Caesarean and Antiochian influences, but instead of the Melkite influence of the eighth century, the Ar-

---

liturgical collection attributed to St. Hippolytus of Rome at the beginning of third century, was preserved only in the oriental traditions. Adaptations of the work have been found in Book 8 of *The Apostolic Constitution* and in *The Testament of the Lord,* a Syrian apocryphon of the fifth century.

menian was influenced by Edessa. The Byzantine and the Armenian rites constitute the Syro-Asiatic branch.

THE EASTERN SYRIAN BRANCH

The Chaldean Rite. This rite, born outside of Hellenism in countries where only Armenian was spoken, appears to have kept more than all others the Semitic characteristics of primitive Christian groups derived from Judaism. Bardesanes, in the second century, and St. Ephrem in the fourth century secured the preponderant influence of Edessa by establishing a repertoire of hymns. This collection passed through all the churches of Syriac language and inspired the Syro-Byzantine melodies. When Antioch reorganized the Persian church at the beginning of the fifth century it probably incorporated the old anaphoras of the Apostles and those which are said to come from Nestorius, and Theodore of Mopsuestia. Between the seventh and the twelfth centuries, the actual repertoire of hymns and prayers of the office and of the ritual were fixed. This was due especially to Catholicos Isoyab III (650–658) and Yahballaha II (1190–1222). The constitution of the Divine Office owes much to the ordinary of the monastery (Dayra Ellayata) of Mossoul.

The Syro-Malabar Rite. The Chaldean rite was spread by the Nestorians far and wide. When the Portuguese arrived in India, this was the rite practiced by the Malabar Christians of St. Thomas, with notable local variations. At the Synod of Diamper (1599), however, under the direction of the Portuguese hierarchy, several Latin usages were introduced into the Syro-Malabar liturgy which thereby lost its primitive purity.

"The East Syrian liturgy is the simplest and most

archaic known to traditional Christianity. It was evolved, and soon reached its fixed form, in surroundings wherein Jewish influences were strong, where from the earliest times Christian communities had a semi-monastic organization, and in an area beyond the Roman world and its exuberant civilization. The territories of the catholicate of Seleucia were never Christian: in Persia, in central Asia and India, the relatively small Christian communities were all but lost in an ocean of infidels. Whatever the factors that conditioned this liturgy, its austerity is striking: the celebration begins with the Lord's Prayer, there are biblical readings and rhythmical homilies, rather like commentaries or glosses, with no rhetorical graces, and these alternate with lengthy monotonous psalmody, the whole taking place in front of a plain wall, with one door, cutting off sight of the altar. As in synagogues, the old churches were dominated by the *bema,* a large platform in the middle of the building; this was the clergy's place, and the lessons were read from it. Sacramental rites are reduced to a minimum and there is little external ceremony, not even in Holy Week, when the rest of Christendom is using those evocative observances that originated in Jerusalem. It is a liturgy of meditation, of listening to the word, of quietness and simplicity—no wonder that it struck an answering note in the souls of the people of India."[5]

THE WESTERN SYRIAN BRANCH

The Syriac Rite. The Syriac rite of the Jacobites is a continuation of the old Greek liturgy of Antioch. Since the Melkites turned to Byzantium and the Maronites, the rite used by the Jacobites best represents the early Anti-

5. Irenée Henri Dalmais, *op. cit.,* p. 59.

ochian liturgy. With its center removed to Mesopotamian Syria, of Armenian culture, this liturgy was made
up of translations of Antiochian Greek liturgy and some
elements from the Syriac repertoire of Edessa. The
Jacobites integrated the hymnal of Severus of Antioch,
which they translated into Syriac; the liturgy was to be
further enriched, until the twelfth century, not only with
hymns but even with anaphoras, thanks to the composition of the Jacobite patriarchs and doctors themselves, and
their adaptations from the Byzantine liturgy. The great
codifiers of the liturgy were Denys Bar Salibi, Bishop of
Amid (1171) and Michael the Great, Patriarch of Antioch (1179).

The Syriac rite penetrated India in the seventeenth century, where it was adopted by the Malabar group and
passed on to the dissident Jacobites, as a result of the
Portuguese lack of understanding. Before the arrival of
the Portuguese, it had belonged to the eastern Syrian rite
and had Nestorian theological leanings.

The Maronite Rite. This is a particular evolution of the
Antiochian rite, developed in the Maronite branch of the
patriarchate of Antioch. Its history during the period preceding the Crusades is little known. Because of renewed
relations with Rome, the Latin influence was more in-
tensely manifested here than in any other oriental Catholic
church; changes in the direction of the Latin appeared
especially in the ritual, in the external symbols and in the
use of unleavened bread. The composition of the Office
and of the Liturgy of the Eucharist remained in conformity
with the rite of Antioch, but more barren than in the
Jacobite branch.

The Antiochian rite is distinguished by its symbolism,
its sense of mystery and of the transcendent. In Antioch

and Jerusalem—these two cities are inseparable in the
history of liturgy—"public worship took on the finest
symbolism: all was directed to the showing forth of an un-
utterable mystery, to making a presence felt. More than
any other, the Syrian liturgy is directed towards the last
things, intent on that Parousia, that Second Coming,
which is already with us through the sacraments. It has
been pointed out how important a part hymns soon had
at Antioch: they deck every celebration in a poetic mantle
which helps the participants to enter into its mystery. From
Jerusalem came those observances, whose symbolism every-
one can understand, which make the decisive moments of
our redemption alive and present to us. The liturgy is in-
tensely human; in this respect very close to that of the
West in the Middle Ages with its spontaneity and drama,
but more successful in keeping the sacred character of its
mystery. Its genius for expressive symbolism reaches its
highest point in Holy Week, but among the Maronites
that has unhappily been spoilt by a feeble naturalism, due
probably to foreign influence."[6]

THE SYRO-ASIATIC BRANCH

The Byzantine Rite. The rite which arose in the Byzantine capital, and which spread throughout the entire
Eastern Orthodox world, is traced back to Syria, with notable influences from Asia Minor. The influence of Antioch
on the capital can be explained, on the one hand, by the
numerous bishops who came from Antioch to occupy the
see of Constantinople during the decisive period from the
fourth to the sixth centuries and on the other hand, by the
far-reaching influence of the pilgrimage centers at the time

6. Irenée Henri Dalmais, *op. cit.*, p. 60.

of the popular feasts which included not only the Holy Lands of Palestine, but also the Basilicas of St. Sergius at Sergiopolis Resafa and of St. Simeon Stylite.

The eucharistic liturgy of St. John Chrysostom, whose oldest manuscript dates back to the eighth entury, is surely of Antiochian origin, and tends to replace the early liturgy of St. Basil, which is perhaps of Egyptian origin, but owes its definitive form to the great Doctor of Caesarea—the liturgy of St. Basil is now celebrated only ten times a year.

The Divine Office dates back, to a great extent, to the influence of the monastery of St. Sabas, near Jerusalem, and to the compositions of the Melkite-Syrian poets. The most celebrated of these poets were: St. Romanus, the Singer, born at Emesa, who lived at the beginning of the sixth century and who was the author of the *kontakia* which were hymns of isosyllabic verse arranged in regular stanzas; St. Andrew of Crete, born at Damascus, monk for a brief time at St. Sabas, who inaugurated the hymno-graphic style of canons which were to replace, in most in-stances, the kontakia. The canon was a series of figures of speech grouped into odes, generally nine, and intended to be inserted between the verses of scriptural hymns of the Office of Matins. He had some illustrious successors, who were also Sabites, such as St. John Damascene and Cosmus of Maiouma. This style passed on to Constantinople along with the liturgical books from the monastery of St. Sabas, and was cultivated by the studious monks who definitively fixed their Byzantine liturgical books.

The Byzantine rite was nearly fixed by the middle of the ninth century, after the victory of Orthodoxy in 842, and the re-establishment of the cult of the icons. How-ever, between the twelfth and the fifteenth centuries, some transformations took place, which burdened and slightly disfigured the primitive beauty of the rite. The prothesis, or preparation of the lay brothers at the beginning of the Mass, was developed out of proportion and constituted a little office by itself; the role of the deacon became preponderant, as the priest recited most of the sacerdotal formulas privately. The Byzantine rite finally took on its present hieratic form which distinguishes it from the other oriental rites.

The extension of the Byzantine rite among the Slavs brought about a few transformations. For a long time the Russians kept the primitive Byzantine form of the tenth century, and did not follow the novelties of Constantinople. In 1654 the Patriarch of Moscow, Nykon, proceeded with several liturgical reforms, in order to put the Russian church in step with the Greek church; this brought about the Schism of the Raskolniks, who insisted on holding to the old traditions. The Melkites who adopted the Byzantine liturgy in the twelfth century, however, allowed a few old customs to subside. At Jerusalem, the early liturgy of St. James is celebrated once a year; we note, too, that the Serbians, the Bulgarians and the Rumanians also have their peculiarities. Despite these differences flowing from the languages used, from musical or architectural style, from rubrics, or from the calendar, the liturgical celebrations of the Russians, the Greeks and the Arabs manifested the fundamental unity of the Byzantine rite, an ecumenical and supranational rite which saw fit to preserve the characteristics proper to each people.

The Byzantine rite inherited from Antioch a taste for ceremonies and hymns; but, when transposed to the capital, it exchanged the cult of the Pantocrator for the imperial pomp of the Court of the basileus. "According to a cherished legend among the Russian people, when the Great Prince Vladimir of Kiev sent ambassadors to Constantinople, the Greek clergy put on a magnificent liturgical display at St. Sophia, in their honor. Upon their return to Kiev, the ambassadors reported as follows to their master: "In the Greek churches, we did not know whether we were in heaven or on earth, for nowhere on earth can such beauty be seen; it is beyond description, and certainly God is there with them, and these Offices are more beautiful than all the Offices of other countries—We can never forget them. Every man who has tasted of sweet things, no longer wants to taste the bitter. Whereupon Prince Vladimir chose for himself and his country the Christianity of Byzantium."[7] The Slavs marked the Byzantine rite with a character more mystical and contemplative, thanks to their serene piety, their meditative icons and their calm and majestic chant.

The Armenian Rite. The constitution of the liturgy of the Armenian church is the result of Caesarean and Edessan influences; its general appearance, however, is from Jerusalem. The formation of this rite ended with a few original compositions, some elements from Byzantium and some Latin contributions from the time of the Crusades. The unique formulary actually used for the eucharistic celebration is an adaptation of the old liturgy of St. Basil.

The resemblance between the Armenian and the Byzantine rites comes from their common dependence upon the early liturgy of Caesarea and from the direct influence of Byzantium on Armenia during the Byzantine domination. The Armenian Office, nevertheless, remained closer

7. According to Gaston Zananiri, in *Histoire de l'Eglise Byzantine,* relying on the Russian chronicle said to be of Nestorius.

to the ancient Asiatic rite since it had not been influenced
by the Melkite monasteries of Palestine. Some Latin customs penetrated, even among non-Catholics, because of the
contacts of the Armenians of Cilicia with the Crusaders.

Despite this, the Armenian rite still conserved its characteristic traits. From antiquity the Armenians were the
only orientals to use the unleavened instead of leavened
bread: they did not mix water with the sacrificial wine.
Their calendar contains very few fixed feasts; in particular,
they have not adopted December 25th, which is of Roman
origin, and have always celebrated Christmas with Epiphany on January 6th. This is what allowed the Armenians
to preserve their personality while all the peoples of Asia
Minor were absorbed and integrated by the Byzantine Empire and the Byzantine church.

"It is by its appointments and singing that the Armenian
liturgy, too, marks its particular quality in the first place.
The absence of a picture-screen, and often even of cur-
tains about the altar, means that one gets the full effect
of the movements of the numerous ministers in their stately
vestments. The liturgy is solemn and recollected, and a
little mournful, qualities that are enhanced by the spe-
cially beautiful chant. The Armenian rite may appear
rather closer than others to us of the Roman rite, because
of its borrowings from the West: but it is also faithful to
the solid sobriety of the ancient liturgy of Caesarea or Antioch before the magnificent but rather overpowering developments of the Byzantine Middle Ages."[8]

THE ALEXANDRIAN LITURGICAL FAMILY

The early liturgy of Alexandria is less known than that
of Antioch because the Alexandrians, being more mystical,

8. Irenée Henri Dalmais, *op. cit.*, p. 61.

have left no descriptions of rites or ceremonies. The only documents available are a prayer book attributed to Serapion of Thmius, Bishop and friend of St. Athanasius (358), and a fragment of liturgy preserved in a manuscript of Deir Balyzeh near Assiout.

After the Monophysite schism, the Melkites continued to use the Greek liturgy, said to be that of St. Mark, but they finally gave it up in the twelfth century in favor of the Byzantine rite. On the other hand, the Monophysites adapted St. Mark's liturgy to Coptic and it developed accordingly; this was the Coptic rite.

The Ethiopians, evangelized by the Syrians, but under Coptic domination which led to their receiving bishops from Egypt, practiced a liturgy which is an affiliate of the Coptic rite, but in their own national tongue, with a more noticeable Syrian influence and their own innovations.

The Coptic Rite. The evolution of the Coptic rite came about in the mold of traditional monasticism, which was so strong in Egypt. Not only the Divine Office, but also the entire eucharistic celebration was marked with a monastic imprint which was reflected in long psalmodies, in its scriptural character, and in its austerity. The influence of the Syrian Jacobites was also preponderant during the Middle Ages. The Copts quickly began to lack vitality, but towards the end of the Middle Ages a realignment took place, when the liturgical books were revised and codified. Two outstanding names related to this work are Abu-Barakat, fourteenth century, and Patriarch Gabriel V. The foreign formularies which had been translated into the ancient dialect, Sahidic, disappeared.

For the eucharistic celebration, the Copts have three liturgies: the one ascribed to St. Cyril, a Coptic adaptation of the Greek liturgy of St. Mark, celebrated once a year; the liturgy of St. Basil abstracted from the Byzantine rite, for the ordinary days; the liturgy of St. Gregory of Nazianzus, for the feasts of Christmas, Epiphany and Easter. Many Syrian customs subsisted in the ritual, but the calendar and the Divine Office kept their traditional appearance despite a few Syrian hymns and some new local productions.

The Coptic liturgy thus appears to be very close to the liturgy of the old monks of the desert. It is excessively slow and drawn out. It shows little external development except for a few expressive gestures, such as the removal of shoes by the celebrants before entering the sanctuary. Together with Coptic, Arabic is used extensively in the celebration of the chants, and some salutations are in Greek. The people participate most fully in the eucharistic action, even during the Canon.

The Ethiopian Rite. This is not a pure translation of the Coptic rite into the classical national tongue, which is Gheez. The liturgy which had come from Egypt developed along the lines of the national character of Ethiopia. Among the seventeen anaphoras gathered from a recent edition of the Missal, we find, next to the adaptations of Coptic anaphoras, those of Syrian origin and even the ancient Roman anaphoras of St. Hippolytus, all of which are blended into a local framework. Ethiopian celebrations were characterized by an ardent and imaginative piety which was contrasted with Coptic austerity. They are profoundly adapted to the spirit of the black races, so different from the Roman spirit.

CONTINUATION AND DEVELOPMENT OF
ORIENTAL LITURGIES

All these liturgies demonstrate, to our envy, how the oriental church saw fit to take root in each human community; consequently, nowhere did the Church appear to be a stranger. It is by being national everywhere that the Church shows herself to be supranational; it is in this variety that her catholicity shows forth. These liturgies, each possessing a repertoire as vast as that of the Roman liturgy, present still unexplored riches and possibilities for adaptation to the different cultures of Asia and Africa.

They can all be traced back to the earliest times and are witnesses to the common faith which existed prior to Christian divisions. In antiquity, never did the question of their legitimacy arise, and never was there a question of precedence of one rite over another. Such things awaited the Middle Ages with its divisive methods. When communion with Rome was interrupted, the oriental liturgies were preserved from the centralizing and unifying efforts which prevailed in the West.

During the Modern Period, the return of western influence has had many repercussions in the liturgical domain. The branches which united with Rome in the heart of each oriental community were able to keep their respective rites.[9] On the one hand, Rome encouraged a positive effort for the scientific study of oriental liturgies, the carefully kept editions of liturgical books, and the preservation of the purity of the rite. On the other hand, some efforts were made to implant the Roman liturgy, and to set up a hierarchy of the Latin rite within oriental territory; this meant creating an additional church community in addition to an established oriental Catholic hierarchy.

This oriental Catholic hierarchy, which depends more on Rome than on the old patriarchs, constantly attempts to

9. During the Middle Ages, the Crusaders adopted a deplorable intransigence to, and an incomprehension of this. The Council of Florence meanwhile had allowed the union in accepting the oriental rites with the rights of the patriarchs.

maintain a liturgical conformity with the corresponding branch not united to Rome. Despite this, numerous customs have infiltrated, which occasionally clash with the spirit proper to the rite, and widen the gap of separation.[10]

The worst repercussion of all was the loss of a liturgical sense. The Latin missionaries, who had been involved at the start of the oriental Catholic branches, and who helped form the spirituality of the clergy and the faithful, often knew little or nothing about the oriental liturgies; they would come into the patriarchate of Antioch as though it were Tonkin or Brazil. They spread a western spirituality cut off from all liturgical roots, including Roman; soon private devotions and pointless hymns multiplied. The laity, like the majority of the clergy trained in Latin seminaries, lost the sense of the liturgy, the taste for the Divine Office, and for solemn Masses; the liturgy was no longer a source of spiritual food adaptable to the soul. The oriental rites were preserved by the Catholic branches, but they were too often merely preserved and not lived in their depth and fullness. The dissatisfaction of a certain class of our faithful for their rite comes from the weighty European influence upon the aristocratic class and from the dwindling of a liturgical sense. If a decadent concept of liturgy has prevailed, a concept which represents liturgy as a formulary or ceremonial of interest mainly to clerics, then men will go to the nearest or richest church.

Another cause of liturgical trouble is the interference of several rites within the same territory of the early Orient. For example, in Syria, besides the Melkite-Byzantine, the Jacobite, and the Maronite branches flowing from the old

10. The matter became even more serious when eastern Catholics were subjected to a Latin hierarchy, as was the case in Malabar and Ethiopia, from the time of the Portuguese until Pius XI.

patriarchal divisions of Antioch, we also find Armenian and Chaldean groups who came from neighboring Armenia and Iraq. Before their union with Rome, all these groups preserved a perfect autonomy among themselves because of their doctrinal differences. For the fractions of these groups united to Rome, the rite remains the only *raison d'être* for the multiplicity of church communities. This is a paradox, however, since the human community must be the support of the church community and the rite, the expression of both of these communities. Wherever there has been national integration and cultural unity, if there is also a unity of faith, there is no longer any need for diversity of church communities or for diversity of rites. We are, therefore, faced with an anomaly, conditioned by all the distinct historical evolution of these communities through the centuries. Moreover, these Catholic communities are transient communities; their permanence is justified in part by the permanence of the separated non-Catholic branches still among them. When Catholic unity becomes a total reality, it will be necessary to bring about a liturgical unity in the interior of Syria by a harmonious and original synthesis of the rites of Antioch and Byzantium.

Rites have been living realities for a long time; some elements have passed away, others have appeared, but they have still remained faithful to themselves. What a great number of hymns and anaphoras have fallen into disuse, are forever lost or merely preserved in manuscripts! The present stage of oriental rites is not an absolute to be preserved at any cost; we must go beyond both Latinism and the spirit of conservation. They are not to be preserved or protected in some treasure chest; they must, freely and viably, adapt themselves to their milieus and go forward. They must be allowed to live and not be hemmed in, to be invigorated by scientific, and historical studies and by a return to the true liturgical spirit; finally, they must be permitted to develop in accordance with the rhythm of new nations that enter the Church.[11]

11. A recent Roman decree imposes on Jews from Israel who wish to become Christians the adherence to the Latin rite and not the Melkite rite, the ancient rite of the country. The Latin patriarchate of Jerusalem, however, owes its existence to the Melkite faithful.

CHAPTER IV · CULTURAL LANGUAGES

Besides hierarchical organization, theological flavor, and rite, cultural language gives diverse oriental churches their own complexion. This applies not only to the reading of the Bible or to the instruction of the faithful but particularly to public worship. The Orient never held to a single language which it considered as sacred. It could have availed itself of the original languages of the Bible or of Apostolic preaching, but it preferred to hold to the language best understood by the faithful, since the people as active members of public worship must grasp the liturgical text in order to respond "Amen." That is why the same rite can be celebrated according to the regions in different languages. Thus the Byzantine rite uses five liturgical languages, namely Greek, Georgian, Staro-Slavonic, Arabic and Rumanian, to mention only the officially recognized ones. Several rites can also be celebrated in the same language: the Chaldean Rite and its Malabar branch, as well as the Syriac and Maronite rites, are all celebrated in the Syriac tongue. Until the eleventh century, before the introduction of local modern languages, the ecclesiastical languages used were: Greek, Syriac, Coptic, Armenian, Georgian, Gheez, Arabic and Staro-Slavonic.

Greek. Greek was the common language in the oriental part of the Roman Empire when Christianity appeared, and it was spoken in Rome and in the valley of the Rhone. This was the language used in the very first Apostolic preaching and in which the books of the New Testament were written; and, ever since the second century before Christ it was the language of the first version of the Old Testament, the Septuagint. That is why Greek was the first language of the Church outside of strictly Jewish and Semitic centers, the language of the Bible and of worship, the language of the Fathers and of the councils. St. Ireneus of Lyons wrote in Greek, as did St. Hyppolitus early in the third century when the liturgy was celebrated in Greek in Rome and in the valley of the Rhone.

The domain of Greek diminished in the West, when it was replaced by Latin under the influence of the Africans and the Spaniards who spoke nothing but Latin. In Syria and in Egypt it gave way to the exclusive use of Syriac, Coptic, and Arabic respectively. Until the ninth century, there were still some Greek writers in Syria such as St. John Damascene, but Greek was less and less understood. The Melkites also abandoned the normal use of Greek in the liturgy and replaced it with Syriac and then with Arabic. The Melkites and the Copts use Greek only sporadically to bolster the ceremonial luster, except in the Hellenic colonies of Alexandria and Jerusalem.

Greek remains the exclusive liturgical language in the patriarchate of Constantinople, the church of Cyprus, the church of Greece and for the Italo-Greeks only. Theoretically the same applies to the oriental Christians of Hungary, as in the diocese of Hajdudorog, but in fact they celebrate the liturgy in Hungarian. In Albania, where Greek is a dead language, it has given way more and more to Albanian; and the Italo-Greeks have become strangers to their liturgical language. The educated Greeks of Istanbul, of Greece, and of Cyprus can understand the simple texts of the liturgy, but the spoken language as well as the written modern language differs quite notably from the old Byzantine Greek. Despite its limited usage, Greek enjoys a considerable prestige, because it still remains the official language of the Bible, of the fathers, and of the Byzantine liturgy.

Syriac. Syriac is the Aramaic literary dialect of Edessa. Aramaic had become the *lingua Franca* in the Middle East ever since the Assyrian period, a few centuries before Alexander introduced Greek into the region. At the time of Christ it was the language spoken by everybody throughout the Fertile Crescent, and in Palestine it had replaced Hebrew. Only the Syrian cities near the Mediterranean spoke Greek. Christ preached in Palestinian Aramaic and it is in this language that St. Matthew wrote his Gospel. This was the language of the first community of Jerusalem before Hadrian reduced the city to a Roman colony in 135; however, it remained in use in the countryside. In a report of his pilgrimage, written at the end of the fourth century, Etherius recalled that after a reading was made in Greek, it was then translated into Syriac. There are still some scriptural texts in Aramaic and some fragments of homilies and liturgical poems utilized by the Melkites of Palestine from the sixth to the ninth century.

Syriac proper, a dialect of Edessa, was to reach far beyond these frontiers. Edessa, whose local dynasty in the first century favored Christianity, rapidly became a very important center of Christian influence in eastern Syria, in Persia, and in Armenia. Immediately after the establishment of Christianity in these countries Syriac became the language of worship. We can trace the first Syriac version of the Old Testament to the middle of the second century. About 175 Tatian, previously a disciple of St. Justin of Rome, composed his *Diatessaron* in Syriac, a summary based on the four Gospels. Early in the third century we find a Syriac version of the separate Gospels and of the New Testament, which no one can trace to a period prior to the *Diatessaron*.

Syriac literature is nearly all Christian and, in a large measure, ecclesiastical. After Tatian, the oldest authors are: Bardesanes (154–222) who wrote *the Dialogue of the Laws of the Countries,* a great philosophical and religious work, and 150 hymns of heterodox flavor; Aphrates, the wise Persian (280–350?) and St. Ephrem. From the fifth to the middle of the seventh century Syriac writers were remarkably prolific, as we see in translations from the Greek and in several original works. The most salient names of this Syriac golden age were: among the Eastern Syrians, Narses (1507) and Babai the Elder (end of the sixth century); among the Western Syrians, Cyrillonus, Isaac of Antioch, and Jacob of Sarug—all three remarkable poets; Philoxenus of Mabbug and John of Ephesus, author of *The Lives of the Saints,* who was a theologian and the best of the Syriac prose writers.

In the sixth century, the Monophysite branch of Antioch gave up Greek in favor of Syriac as its official tongue, as did the Maronite branch in the seventh century. But the dialect of Western Syrians, of the Jacobites and Maronites, drifted slightly away from that of the eastern Syrians, the Nestorians of the church of Persia, by way of pronunciation of certain vowels and in the form of writing. The Melkites also used Syriac in their villages until the sixteenth century.

After the conquest of the Arabs Syriac remained very much alive until the ninth century, as we learn from the writings of James of Edessa for the Jacobites and from those of the Catholicos, Timotheus, for the Nestorians. But Arabic was spoken more and more as many of the writers became bilingual. The last great writers belonged to the twelfth and thirteenth centuries; among these were: Denys Bar Salibi, the Exegete (1171); Michael the Syrian, the Chronicler (1179); Bar Hebreus (1284) who excelled in all directions; all three Jacobites; and Ebd Jesus (1318), a Nestorian canonist. There is some evidence that Syriac was spoken as late as the seventeenth century. A few villages near Damascus still use an Aramaic dialect, while the Chaldean Christians of Kurdistan and of Mesopotamia speak a dialect derived from Syriac, called Soureth.

As a liturgical language, Syriac is used today by the Maronites, by the Catholic Syrians and the Jacobites of the patriarchates of Antioch and of India, by the Eastern Syrians, by the Catholic Chaldeans or Nestorians, and by the Malabarese. The Western Maronites and Syrians make a limited use of Arabic, written in Syriac characters called carshuni. This usage had been requested for the Maronites by the Synod of Mt. Libanus in 1736 and for Catholic Syrians by the Synod of Charf in 1888. The eastern Syrians were more strict; only the scriptural pericopes were read in Arabic in the large cities, since the people who spoke Soureth generally understood the classical Syriac which they had learned in school. In India Syriac is not understood by the people, so that the Jacobites by and large use Malayan, the local tongue of Malabar. Their branch, the Syro-Malankarese, which became Catholic in 1930, did the same. The Malabarese, or Catholics of the Latinized eastern Syrian rite, influenced by the Decree of the Council of Trent forbidding the living language, used Syriac only until 1962 when they reintroduced Malayan into the liturgy with Roman approbation.

Coptic. Coptic is the last evolution in the language of the pharaohs which was deeply influenced by Greek. Coptic, here, is understood to be Egyptian. It is made up, principally, of two dialects which are: Sahidic in northern Egypt from an older literary usage and Bohairic in the Delta. Outside of the Greek cosmopolitan city of Alexandria, Hellenism had spread only superficially in Egypt where the mass of Fellaheen knew little or no Greek. As soon as Christianity was established in the country, translations of the Sacred Scriptures into Coptic began to appear. It is interesting to note that the Young Anthony, born in 251, was converted while listening to the reading of the Gospels, which must have been in Coptic since he understood nothing else. After the Monophysite schism, while the Melkites held on to Greek, the Monophysites abandoned it more and more in favor of Coptic.

Coptic literature had its brief popularity during the fifth and sixth centuries and then faded rapidly with the Arab invasion, because Egypt did not have any important cultural center except Alexandria which was predominantly Greek. Precious little remains of early Coptic literature, except for some translations, some lives of Egyptian saints, some aphorisms of the Fathers of the Desert and some disciplinary canons. There was only one, original author of importance, whose name was Senout. After the ninth century principal writings were in Arabic; the last Coptic writing was found in the twelfth century. Coptic is no longer spoken. To the best of our knowledge, the last old man who understood it died in the seventeenth century. Consequently, in their liturgy the Copts use Arabic, but on some occasions Coptic is used with Greek as the language of pomp.

Armenian. Armenian is an Indo-European language. Since Christianity came into Armenia via Edessa and later via Caesarea of Cappadocia with Gregory the Illuminator, both Syriac and Greek influences have intermingled from the very beginning.

At the end of the fourth century Armenia fell into the hands of the Persians who forbade the use of Greek and wanted to impose Syriac as the liturgical language everywhere in imitation of the church of Persia. The Catholicos Sahok III, the Great (390–440), in order to prevent the integration of Armenia into the Persian Empire, published a national alphabet, with the help of the monk, Mesrob, and organized a team of translators who enriched Armenia with the Christian literature it so badly needed. Translations started with Syriac and Greek, and helped philologists to trace some primitive texts, as for example, part of St. Ireneus' work the original of which had been lost. Some original works were also produced; among the writers of these we find the following important authors: In theology, Eznik in the fifth century; in history, Agathangelus and Moses of Khoran in the fifth century; in religious poetry, Gregory of Narek, et al. This literature has been studied very little.

Since the Armenians generally succeeded in preserving their national tongue, modern Armenian hardly differs from the classical Armenian. A large number of faithful of the Armenian Church, however, separated from its center, no longer understand its language. For instance, the Armenian community of Lvov in Poland speaks only Polish; the Armenians who inhabited Cilicia before the Great War spoke Turkish only; those of Mardin spoke

Arabic; and, since the seventeenth century the early Armenian colony of Aleppo has spoken only Arabic. The new wave of immigrants at the time of the massacres of Turkey speaking Armenian or Turkish were a group apart, and thus posed an administrative problem for the Armenian episcopacy of Aleppo.[1]

The use of Armenian in the liturgy remains very strict. The synod of Armenian Catholics held in Rome in 1911 permits the reading of scriptural pericopes in the local tongue but only after a reading in classical Armenian and without the same ceremonies. The Catholic Armenians of Aleppo are more lenient towards Arabic, because of the influence of the Melkites, the Syriacs, and the Maronites; the other Armenian communities of Lebanon and Syria wish they, too, could do the same.

Georgian. Georgian is the language of the Caucasian group, probably allied to the Basques; it is neither Semitic nor Indo-European. When Christianity spread into Georgia about the fourth or fifth century, through the efforts of missionaries from Antioch, its rulers were allied to Armenia; Georgia was therefore subjected to both Greco-Syrian and Armenian influences. The Old Georgian version of the Bible, which dates back to the fifth century, seems to be based on a Greek or Armenian text derived from Syriac—although specialists do not agree on this question. By the end of the sixth century, the break with Monophysite Armenia was complete, as the Georgians declared themselves unequivocally in favor of the dogma of Chalcedon.

1. It was especially so for the Catholics for whom the two linguistic elements were the same in parts. Among the non-Catholics, the Old Arab element already of little importance, was submerged by the mass of immigrants, the great majority of whom were non-Catholics.

Before the eleventh century Georgia enjoyed close ties with the Melkites of Syria. The patriarch of Antioch had a right of allegiance over Georgia; and the Georgian liturgy and calendar were closely dependent on those of Jerusalem. We note here that the monks in Melkite territory, at Sinai, in Jerusalem at the Holy Cross, and near Antioch on the Black Mountain translated a number of Greek, Syrian, and Arabic works into Georgian. When the Arabic grip had been relaxed in the eleventh century, Georgia recovered a certain independence under King David, the Restorator, and Queen Thamar. She then turned towards Byzantium. Earlier, St. John and St. Euthymeus had founded the Iviron Monastery on Mount Athos, which became the home of great Georgian religious culture and an important translation center. Georgian literature is, in fact, principally one of translation in which we find the following outstanding names: Euthymeus the Athonite (1028), George the Athonite (1066), Ephrem the Minor (1100) and Arseneus of Iqualto (1140). The monks of Mt. Athos have preserved many patristic works which constitute valuable hagiography; unfortunately these works have not yet been thoroughly categorized and the manuscripts are not easily accessible.

Like the Melkites, the Georgians adopted the Byzantine liturgy in the eleventh century, which they translated into Georgian from that time on. The Russians who have lived in Georgia since the end of the eighteenth century have tried to impose Slavonic in order to assimilate the country. The Georgians, however, continue to celebrate the liturgy in their national tongue, which has not changed much and which is understood by the people.

Geez. Geez is the classical language of Ethiopia; it belongs to the Semitic group and closely resembles the

Arabic of the South. With the help of Syrian missionaries
Christianity spread into Ethiopia during the fourth century, and the Axum Kingdom, comprising northern Ethiopia, became officially Christian. In the sixth century an
expedition in southern Arabia brought help to the persecuted Christians; but, at the start of the next century, the
first Meccan followers of Mohammed, who were persecuted by the idolators, went to the Christian king of
Ethiopia to seek refuge. It is to this period that a Bible,
taken from the Greek and Syriac versions, can be traced.
Ethiopia soon felt the influence of Egypt and followed the
Monophysitism of the Coptic church.

Starting with the seventh century, Ethiopia went
through an obscure period, and it was not until the thirteenth century that literary activity began anew, last-
ing until the seventeenth century. As might be expected,
it was a work of translation and of compilation dependent
upon Arabic literature of Egypt, since Coptic was already
dead. There remain, however, a few original works and
liturgical poems; among these, the important ones are: *The
Research* of Zara Yakob in the fifteenth century, *Reflex-
ions on Religion; The Book of Mysteries* fifteenth century,
Refutation of Heresies; and *The Acts of Philmona,* saint of
the fourteenth century. Ethiopian literature is essentially
a popular literature which reflects the soul and religious
needs of the Ethiopian people. Its golden age was during
the reign of Emperor Zara Yakob (1434–1468).

At the outset of the sixteenth century, the Emperor
Lebna Denghel appealed to the Portuguese for help to
repel the Moslem invasion; help was granted and with
it came Catholic missionaries. The Jesuits who tended
to impose the Roman liturgy translated into Geez, and to
introduce Latin customs, were routed in the year 1636.

For a long time thereafter Ethiopia remained closed to the West and fell into decadence. Today, a new and interesting challenge lies ahead for Ethiopia. Geez has not been spoken since the sixteenth century; it has been replaced by two Semitic languages, Tigriña and Amharic, both influenced by African dialects. It remains, however, a sacred language understood only by the elite. The liturgy is celebrated in Geez, and, to the best of our knowledge, no action has yet been taken in favor of changing to a living language.

Arabic. Long before the advent of Islamism, Christianity had penetrated the Arab world. The Ghassanid kingdom, protecting the Byzantine border and maintaining contact with Syria, was Monophysite; Prince Al Harith was the great protector of Jacob Baradai. The Lakhmid Kingdom, on the Persian border, was Nestorian, with Hira as center, and several Nestorian episcopates were set up along the Arabian coastline of the Persian Gulf and in Oman. A Christian community was organized in Yemen, with a center at Najran, where Persian and Ethiopian influences intermingled. During this period, there was no indication that these truly Arabic, Christian communities, which did not long withstand Islamism, had had any Christian literature in their own national language. We do know, however, that the language used for correspondence was either Syriac or Greek; hence, if there were any translations, they must have been oral ones.

A Christian Arabic literature was born among the arabicized Christians of Iraq, of Syria and of Egypt within the Arab Empire. A translation movement was started in the eighth century when some writings were composed for the intention of Christians and others for the Moslem Arabs. The oldest Christian author seems to have been

Theodore Abuqurra, Melkite Bishop of Harran, who died about the year 825.[2] Starting with the tenth century, Arabic seems to have gained prominence over the old national languages; it became a new *Koine* for Nestorians, Jacobites, Melkites, Maronites, and Copts. As might be expected, the most rapid arabicizing occurred in the cities and in the great plains.

Besides an abundant literature of translation comprising patristic and conciliar texts, as well as apocryphal and hagiographical tales, there were some original Arabic writings during the eighth to the thirteenth century; these were chiefly chronicles, a few theological encyclopedias and controversies with Moslems and those of other confessions. The outstanding authors of this period were the following:

Nestorians. Elias of Nisibis in the eleventh century, a chronicler and controversialist; Mari Ibn Suleiman in the twelfth century, author of a theological encyclopedia, *The Book of the Tower.*

Jacobites. Yahya Ben Adi in the tenth century, Christian philosopher, author of apologies addressed to the Moslems; Bar Hedrus (1284), author of *The History of the Dynasties,* who was also a prolific Syriac writer.

Melkites. Theodore of Abuqurra, Bishop of Harran (736–825?) author of apologies and controversies addressed to Moslems, to Monophysites, and to Nestorians; Eutychius, known as Said Ibn Al Bitriq, Patriarch of Alexandria (940), author of a well-known chronicle; Abdallah Ibn Al Fadi, Deacon of Antioch in the eleventh

2. There were some names in Arabic literature prior to Abuqurra, but they were related to secular poetry, such as Al Akhtal (710) the celebrated cantor of Ommiads. The homily attributed to Qouss Ibn Saïda, Bishop of Najran in Yemen, at the end of the sixth century, seems to be apocryphal.

century, translator and encyclopedist; Paul, Bishop of Sidon, a thirteenth-century controversialist.

Maronites. Thomas of Kafar Tab in the eleventh century.

Copts. Severus of Asmounein in the tenth century and Ibn Al Moqaffat, both controversialists; Abu-L-Barakat, author of *The Book of the Lamp of Darkness,* a dogmatic summary.

From the fourteenth to the nineteenth century the Arabic East went through a period of obscurity, while it was ruled by Mongols and Turks; yet, in the seventeenth century a certain renaissance appeared among Christians after the arrival of Western missionaries. The new Christian Arabic literature, of which Lebanon is the most important center, is heavily influenced by the West, and is still trying to find itself.

As we have seen, Arabic was gradually introduced into the liturgy, and encroached upon Greek, Syriac, and Coptic. The most arabicized liturgy is that of the Melkites. We find the liturgy of St. John Chrysostom in an Arabic manuscript of the eleventh century. Among the Melkites the divine worship may be celebrated entirely in Arabic. On some occasions, always optional and for the sake of greater solemnity, they include a few commonly used formulas of the Greek liturgy. The Copts also make use of Arabic, but the Syriacs and the Maronites are more strict, and the Chaldeans permit it only in the reading of the scriptural pericopes.

Liturgical Arabic is the literary Arabic, which, although it differs from the spoken language, is still understood by all and is the only one used in the newspapers, on radio, and in books. It deserves a wider usage in the liturgy, not only in the Near East but also in North Africa. Interest-

ingly enough, the Little Brothers and Little Sisters of Jesus
have adopted the Melkite Arabic liturgy not only for their
eastern houses but also for those of Algeria and Morocco.
Would it not lead to a profound spiritual rapprochement
with Islamism, if we prayed in its sacred tongue?

Staro-Slavonic. The introduction of Slavonic as a liturgical language is due to two oriental missionaries, St. Cyril
and St. Methodius, who arrived in Moravia shortly before
864. With a command of at least a Slavonic dialect they
composed a special alphabet adapted to Slavonic sounds,
called Glagolitic, through which they translated the Bible
and some parts of the Byzantine and the Roman liturgy.
Strong opposition came forth from neighboring Germans,
who wanted to maintain the use of Latin and to introduce
Moravian into their religious and political spheres of influence. The two apostles succeeded in having their work
approved in 869 by Pope Hadrian II, who consecrated
Methodius Archbishop of Pannonia with jurisdiction over
all of Moravia. St. Cyril died in Rome while this was
taking place. Despite his episcopal rank and jurisdiction
Methodius was imprisoned by the Germans and badly
mistreated. Pope John VIII re-established him in his see
and, after condemning the use of Slavonic in 879, au-
thorized it in 880. Methodius died in peace in 885.

Wiching, his German adversary, hurried to Rome, and
armed with a false letter from John VIII, obtained the
condemnation of Slavonic from Stephen V, thereby ruin-
ing the work of Methodius for the Slavs of the West.
Some of his disciples went to Dalmatia and preserved the
Roman liturgy in Slavonic Glagolitic; this usage was to be
approved in 1248 by Innocent IV, thanks to the prestige
of St. Jerome, native of Dalmatia, to whom this liturgy
was henceforth attributed. The majority of Methodius'

disciples fled to Bulgaria, where they were welcomed by the Czar, Simeon. Thanks to a modification of Greek uncials in the eighth century, they forged a new alphabet, falsely called Cyrillic with which they translated the various books of the Byzantine liturgy into Slavonic. Staro-Slavonic soon became the liturgical language of all the Slavs of the Byzantine rite, including Russians, Belo-Russians, Ukrainians, Serbians, and Bulgarians. It was also used by the Rumanians until the sixteenth century. During that same period it was the language of the educated and the intellectuals among the Slavs, except the Poles.

Today, Staro-Slavonic is a dead language; the modern Slavonic languages differ from it in various ways. Russian is the language closest to it; hence a Russian of moderate culture can easily follow the most common parts of the liturgy. The next closest is Ukranian which differs only slightly from Russian; then Bulgarian, which derives basically from Staro-Slavonic, and, finally, Serbian.

The Rumanians, whose Slavonic culture was forged during the Middle Ages when they united with the Bulgarians, lost this culture when the Bulgarian Empire fell into the hands of the Ottomans. Slavonic, no longer understood during the fifteenth century even among the clergy, was gradually replaced by Rumanian during the sixteenth century. It was still written in Cyrillic characters as late as the nineteenth century, but since then Latin characters have been used, and all vestige of Slavonic culture has disappeared from Rumania.

Staro-Slavonic has nonetheless remained as the liturgical language most commonly used in the Orient. "In this sacred dialect, the piety of the people finds a tongue closely enough related to make it transparent, sufficiently different, and old enough to lend more solemnity to divine worship."[3]

THE MODERN LANGUAGES

The languages we have treated above are not exclusive, for others were used from Antiquity through the Middle Ages as need dictated. In the fourth century Bishop Goth Ulphilas translated the Bible for the Germans who had settled on the coast of the Black Sea. Besides Syriac, known as *pahlevi* or old Persian, Turkish *ouigour* and Chinese were also used in the Persian church and in its missions. In the twelfth century, Balsamon, the Byzantine Patriarch of Antioch, replied to Mark, Patriarch of Alexandria, who was concerned about Armenian and Syrian priests who had not embraced Monophysitism and who celebrated the liturgy in their own language. He formulated the following oriental principle in that reply: "Those who are Orthodox in all things, but who are entirely ignorant of the Greek language, will celebrate in their own tongue, provided they have error-free copies of the customary prayers translated from scrolls in well-written Greek letters." This principle has had many applications in the Modern Era, as we note from the following:

In oriental Europe, the nations which did not understand Staro-Slavonic or Greek, introduced their national language into the liturgy.

——For the *Rumanians* this is an accomplished fact since the seventeenth century.

——*Hungarian* is already utilized in the oriental Catholic

3. Anatole Leroy-Baulieu, *L'Empire des Tsars et les Russes,* Vol. III, *La Religion,* p. 86.

diocese of Hajdudorog with tacit approval of Rome. The condemnation of Hungarian in 1896 was never put into effect.

——*Albanian* is spreading more and more in Albania without having completely replaced Greek.

——Some celebrations have been permitted in *Estonian, Lettish, Polish, Ukranian* and *Finnish.*

——The Russians have not hesitated to translate the liturgy in their missions into the local languages, such as, *Tatar* in Central Asia, *Chinese, Japanese* and the dialect of the *Eskimos.*

——The Jacobite-Malabarese have tended to replace Syriac with *Malayan,* which is the language of southern India.

In the emigrant oriental colonies of western Europe and in America, the tendency is to use English, French, Spanish, or Portuguese according to the needs of the faithful The oriental authority does not object to the existing evolution which is quite natural and in the spirit of oriental discipline. In fact, it assists and directs this evolution, and therefore deserves the confidence of Rome.[4]

4. In December, 1959, in the name of the Holy Office, oriental priests in Europe and in America were forbidden to utilize, even in part, the existing modern language in celebrating the liturgy. Maximos IV Saigh, Melkite Patriarch of Antioch, in a letter dated February 5, 1960, confronted Pope John XXIII with the question. On March 31, of the same year, the Holy Office, repealing its decisions, permitted the use of the mother tongue in the Byzantine rite, except for the canon. It seems to us that the oriental principle of the aptitude of all languages to serve for divine worship can be applied to the integral text of the liturgy. (*P.O.C.* 1960, pp. 134, 135.)

B Y A STRANGE PARADOX the oriental church, so profoundly
embodied in the human, was disengaged from this
world. Essentially eschatological and liturgical, it was destined to be little influenced by time and history in its life
and internal structures; in fact, from a dogmatic and disciplinary viewpoint, the oriental church hardly ever changed.
However, Christian as well as Moslem princes often inserted themselves into religious affairs, because the boundaries of the profane and the sacred had been poorly drawn.
Oriental Christianity, therefore, in its external form and its
numerical and political importance, strongly resented the
periodic reverses in history through which she was forced
to live.

In antiquity the Roman Empire subjected both East
and West to a unique regime. The division of the empire
under Diocletian and especially after Theodosius prepared
the upheavals of the Middle Ages; Constantinople became
Hellenized and Rome became Latinized. All the while in
both capitals, the same family ruled; the unity of the
Roman Empire remained. But Roman influence was to

77

be broken by the German and Arab assaults; from this
rupture came forth the world of the Middle Ages. Yet, the
invasions were not the only cause of dislocation; in the
East, one century before the advent of Islamism, the religious secession of Egypt and Syria gave proof of the dis-
affection which these nations had toward the empire,
and prepared the way for the political separation of the
seventh century. In the West the German barbarians, for
a long time, considered themselves as agents of the Roman
Empire. Clovis was flattered to receive the honorary title
given to him by Anastasius, Emperor of the East, and,
in the meantime, Justinian regained possession of Rome
and a portion of the West. The decline of Roman influence was consummated when Rome passed from the
tutelage of Byzantium to that of Pepin, and especially
when the pope crowned Charlemagne, a barbarian, Emperor of the Romans.

Henceforth the old Roman world was separated into
three rival blocks:

The Arabic Califate, which comprised, over and above
Arabia, all of the southern coastline of the Mediterranean,
eastern Asia Minor, Syria and Egypt, northern Africa and
Spain, and the early Persian Empire. Therein lay the political power of Islamism. Arabic became the common cultural language.

The Eastern Roman Empire, or Byzantine Empire,
which was reduced to Asia Minor and the Balkans, and
which is still disputed by the Bulgarians and the Slavs.
The only thing Roman which remains is the name, because it is, in fact, a Greek empire. Russia depends on this
empire for its spirituality; Orthodoxy and Byzantine liturgy unite all of these peoples spiritually.

Western Christianity comprised, over and above the

early Western Roman Empire, exclusive of Africa and Spain, all of the Germanic territories. The center of gravity left the Mediterranean countries linked to the East, and displaced itself to the North, in the heart of the Germanic countries. This dislocation was caused by the economic decadence of Italy and Provence, which was due to the Arabic hegemony in the Mediterranean and to the military power of the conquerors of the empire. This Western world, with its two heads, emperor and pope, bore well its name of Holy Roman Germanic Empire.

The above divisions were to have grave consequences for the unity of the Church. They were to harden the divisions of the seventh century. Inasmuch as Syria and Egypt depended on the empire, an effort was made to bridge the schism, but the Arabs preferred to see the Christians divided, and to maintain the religious split between their Christian subjects and the Orthodox of the rival empire. A new moat was dug between the Orthodox East and the West. Even after the fall of the Roman Empire in the West, Rome had held on to ties with the East; the Latin peoples remembered their common life with the East and did not feel like total strangers to oriental traditions. The Germans, on the contrary, who were to dominate the Western world, were newcomers who had never had any contact with the orientals. The Byzantines, limited to Greek-speaking countries alone, became more and more Hellenized; they looked upon themselves as a continuation of Roman antiquity and the trustees of tradition, animated with a certain superiority complex toward the West, which had fallen prey to the barbarians. The papacy, linked to the Germanic Empire, no longer appeared as a universal spiritual primacy, but as a tool of the Western world. To have accepted submission to a papacy

represented by a Gregory VII or an Innocent III would
have been tantamount to recognizing the suzerainty of a
Germanic Roman Empire.

These wounds have not yet healed in the Modern Era,
despite the fact that the world is tending to become more
unified. Therefore, we shall consider successively the evolution of the churches, first in the Arab block and then in
the Byzantine-Slavonic block before touching upon the
vicissitudes of East-West relations.

CHAPTER V · THE CHURCH
IN THE ARAB WORLD

The Arabic invasion did not ruin the Church's existence in the Orient as it had done in northern Africa; but thirteen centuries of an Islamic theocracy gradually ate away its effectiveness and choked its cultural and spiritual expansion. Cut off from all relations with the rest of Christendom, living in the Arabic world as in a ghetto, deprived of all action on the politico-social front, and reduced to its liturgical function, the church of the Arabic East lost the role of first place which it had enjoyed for the first six centuries. But its potentialities remained latent; as soon as the first glimpse of freedom appeared and normal relations with the rest of Christendom could be re-established, the church of the ancient patriarchates once again played its unequalled role despite its reduced effectiveness. This church which had kept alive the oldest Christian traditions and survived through thirteen centuries of oppression and persecution, deserves all of our esteem and attention.

The preservation of Christian life in the East can be considered a moral miracle. Why did the Church succeed in staying alive in the Orient, while it fell apart in Africa? The Arabs were more tolerant than the Berbers, true; but, in the Orient, the faith had grown much deeper roots. The patriarchal organization gave the Christians a very effective status, and a religious, as well as a quasi-national structure. The numerous monasteries which survived during the previous era had preserved the Christian culture at a respectable level for several centuries. Finally, the liturgy in a living language, and rich in doctrine and expressive ceremonies, succeeded in nourishing the faith and piety of the faithful.[1]

GENERAL STATUS OF CHRISTIANS IN ISLAMIC COUNTRIES

The Moslem regime allowed the Christians freedom of worship, except for a few restrictions, but did not concede to them a right of citizenship equal to that of the Moslems. They were not allowed to bear arms, were subject to a special tax, and were plagued by vexations and annoyances. The fanaticism and rapacity of the rulers fell on them in arbitrary opposition to the law which, in itself, was more tolerant.

Since the state was theocratic, Christians could not be constrained to follow all the laws. Various Christian communities were legally recognized, and were interiorly ruled in all personal matters according to their own laws under the authority of their respective patriarchs. As a result, this state of affairs hardened the Christian divisions and gave an appearance of quasi-national communities to the various churches, which made Christian unity a particularly delicate problem in the Arabic East.

1. Among the causes of the disappearance of Christianity in northern Africa we must point out in particular the weakening of this church due to Donatism and the colonial character of Christianity assumed in northern Africa.

Christians were still in the majority during the great Arab period until the eleventh century. Despite their rank of second-class citizens they played a significant role in the formation of Arabic civilization; from an economic and technical standpoint, they were the backbone of the empire. On the cultural side they initiated the Arabs to the Greek language; through Arabic translations or the intermediary of Syriac, they transmitted the basic elements of Greek philosophy, medicine, mathematics, astronomy and physics. Many Christians held high positions in the administration, and others became famous in Arabic literary circles. An Islamo-Christian dialogue was started under the leadership of the enlightened Calif, Almanoun (813–833), but the fierce reaction of Al Mutawadil (847–861) put an end to these happy relations. From a purely Christian point of view, the church kept its old organizations and personnel. The monasteries, still numerous, maintained a certain level of culture and produced many theological writings worthy of interest: among others, the work of St. John Damascene dates back to a century after the Arabic occupation.

Toward the end of this period the Byzantine emperors of the Macedonian Dynasty succeeded in reconquering Edessa (944), Cilicia, the region of Antioch (968), and Armenia (1024). This momentary recapture hastened the coalescence of the Melkite church with the Byzantine, but deepened the gap between the Armenians and the Jacobites, on the one hand, and the Byzantine church on the other. In fact, the Armenians and the Jacobites bitterly resented the efforts of the Byzantines to bring them back to the faith of Chalcedon.

The Seljuk Turks captured the lands conquered by the Byzantines, after the Battle of Malazkirt in 1071 and drove them almost completely out of Asia Minor. The destruction of the brilliant Christian communities of Asia Minor dates back to this era; the last remnants were to be liquidated by the Turks during the War of 1914–1918 and after. Starting from the eleventh century, the Turks had the upper hand in the Arab world. This brought about a general decline of culture and the impoverishment of the country, because of wars, revolts, and negligence of the rulers. The Turks were far less tolerant than the Arabs. The cruelties suffered by westerners who went there on pilgrimages gave rise to the great adventure of the Crusades, which poisoned the relations between the Moslems and the oriental Christians for a long time. If the West first benefited from renewed contacts with the birthplace of Christianity, the East, during the obscure centuries weighing heavily upon it, would also profit from the Western overture. To this extent, the Crusades had, as a happy result, the reestablishment of a bridge between the two worlds.

The Crusaders left the conquered lands of the Syrian West, and a country ruined by war. After them came the Mongols in the second half of the thirteenth century, sowing blood and fire; then came the second invasion, still more terrible, of Tamerlane in 1400. All of these misfortunes weakened the eastern churches considerably, and Christians were henceforth to be numerically insignificant. For the most part the monasteries were destroyed and Christian culture was reduced to a mere shadow. In 1516 Syria fell under the pressure of the Ottomans, who already ruled Constantinople; the following year, it was Egypt's turn. The early eastern empire seemed to be unified once again; however, it was not the Pax Romana, but the worse regime of vexations and arbitrariness ever to confront the Christian world.

While the new spirit hovered over Europe, the church of the Orient knew its darkest hours; nevertheless, the dawn of the Renaissance began to break through. The capitulations, signed between Francis I and Soliman, gave France a certain right to the protection of the Christian minorities, subjects of the sultan. The new consulates which were set up, and the arrival of missionaries, especially in the seventeenth century with the Franciscans, the Jesuits, the Carmelites, the Capuchins, the Lazarists and the Dominicans, renewed contact with the West. The schools founded in Rome for the orientals by Pope Gregory XIII, such as the Greek College of St. Athanasius in 1576 and the Maronite College in 1584, produced a large number of oriental priests who were to be the pioneers of the spiritual renewal in their countries. During the seventeenth and eighteenth centuries, some erudite scholars became interested in the Orient.

The life of Christians in the Ottoman Empire remained the same nevertheless; reforms of the Sultan Abdulmajid (1839–1861), guaranteeing equality to Ottoman citizens, Moslem or Christian, were dead letters. A new wind began to blow, however, during the nineteenth century when Arabic nationalism was awakened; first came a renaissance of Arabic culture, then a vindication of freedom and autonomy. Christians were to play a preponderant role in this renewal, and were thus to integrate themselves into the national life.

The defeat of 1918 put an end to Turkish domination in Arabic countries; however, the newly established states did not obtain complete independence immediately. The

passing mandates of England for Egypt,[2] Palestine, Transjordan and Iraq, and of France for Syria-Lebanon cooled
relations between the Moslems and the Christians, for
the latter, being generally more cultured, acquired important governmental posts, whereas shortly before, during
the Turkish Era, they had been considered as second-rate
citizens. The Christians, nevertheless, always demonstrated
true patriotism and cooperated in the full liberation of
the country.

In the new modern Arabic states the principle of equality between Moslems and Christians was established, but
integration of the two groups was not completely realized
and equality was not absolute. Because of various religious
persuasions, the law prevailed in Lebanon, where public
functions were wisely apportioned among the different religious communities. Elsewhere, the regime was inspired
by Moslem law; Islam observed no distinction between
church and state, and despite official declarations the average citizen deliberately confused Islamism with nationalism. Christian communities still kept their former juridical
personality. A religious marriage, for instance, whether
Moslem or Christian, was sanctioned by law. Catholics
were not allowed divorce; in the event of a separation, the
food pension to be paid to dependents was fixed by an ecclesiastical tribunal. Yet, although the state allowed Islamism to function freely, it did not recognize the conversion
of a Moslem to Christianity. A convert could not legally
marry in the Church, since, before the law, he was still
a Moslem, and since civil marriage did not exist, he was
compelled to recognize Moslem authority and to register
his children as Moslems.

2. Egypt had been a protectorate since 1882.

We do not know what the future holds, since the Arab world is in the midst of a full evolution and torn by opposing ideals—between socialism or democracy on the one hand, and classical Islamism on the other.

PARTICULAR EVOLUTION OF VARIOUS CHURCHES

The Melkites. At the time of the Arabic conquest many Melkites left their country with the Byzantine troops; those who remained suffered a less favorable fate than that of other Christians because of their ties with Byzantium. For a long time the patriarchal sees of Alexandria, Antioch, and Jerusalem were vacant; in fact, they were not filled until the eighth century. The Melkites were especially numerous in the patriarchates of Antioch and Jerusalem. In Egypt, they were lost in a Moslem and Coptic mass, and had only one bishop besides the patriarch. In Damascus, capital of the Ommiads, they occupied high ranks in the administration. They also kept several seeds of culture until the time of the Crusades, notably the monasteries in the vicinity of Antioch, such as those of St. Simeon the Younger, St. Sabas, and St. Chariton near Jerusalem, and the celebrated monastery of St. Catherine in Sinai. During the eighth and ninth centuries they produced a proliferation of theologians and hymnographers whose works passed on through Byzantine tradition, and who were ardent defenders of Orthodox faith against the Iconoclast Emperors. Among these great theologians St. John Damascene deserves the first place.

In the tenth century Antioch fell under Byzantine domination for a century and a quarter. During this period the patriarchate of the Melkites came under the jurisdiction of the ecumenical patriarch; several patriarchs were chosen from the clergy of the capital and were named by the emperor. The Crusades would end the Byzantine influence and control of the Melkite patriarchates. In fact, the Crusaders established Latin patriarchs in the sees of Antioch and Jerusalem; they placed the Melkite bishoprics under the wing of these new titulars. Meanwhile the legitimate Melkite ordinaries escaped to Constantinople where they remained for nearly two centuries. The Melkites were disrupted by the Crusaders; the other communities, perhaps because they did not have the same faith as the Latins, were able to retain their hierarchies.

Antioch was ruined in 1268 by the Mameluk sultan, Baibars; the other Frankish colonies were liquidated in 1291. Cilicia still remained under Armenian rule until its fall in 1375; the patriarchs were to reside here, for Cilicia was part of the patriarchate of Antioch. Then, following an agreement between the Byzantine and Mameluk emperors who belonged to the Circassian, Turkish Dynasty residing in Cairo and ruling Syria, they settled in Damascus.

The Church was beaten to death by the Crusades and the Mongolian invasion. As a result, the history of the patriarchates from the fourteenth to the seventeenth century is obscure and mixed with intrigue. We know that during the fifteenth century the patriarchs were represented at Florence and renewed relations with Rome; in fact, the Melkite church never broke its ties with Rome. The conciliatory attitude of the Patriarch of Antioch, Peter III, in the fight between Cerularius and the pope, is well known; but the subjection of the Melkites to the Byzantine patriarch because of these rough times dragged them into a split with Rome. In 1516, when the country fell into the hands of the Ottomans, the Melkite patriarchates were again subjects of the patriarch of Constantinople by order of the sultan. The sees of Alexandria and Jerusalem were taken by the Greeks, who still retain possession of them.

The patriarchate of Antioch stayed in the hands of nationals until 1724, when a split occurred between the Catholic element and those opposed to union with Rome. The Catholics allowed the existent national patriarchs to continue; the Orthodox received a Greek patriarch and were under Greek influence until 1898, when the national element regained the upper hand with the help of the Russian church. Catholic patriarchs were no longer permitted to reside in Damascus since they were considered to be enemies of the Orthodox hierarchy, the only one recognized by the sultan; so they escaped to Lebanon. The Catholics of Syria, who suffered countless annoyances, shed their blood at Aleppo in 1818.

The war of Greek independence weakened the hopes of the Greeks at Istanbul. The occupation of Syria by Mehemet Ali also engendered a certain freedom. The Melkite Patriarch, Maximus III Mazloum, succeeded in returning to Damascus in 1834, and obtained from the Sultan the complete civil emancipation of the Catholics from the Orthodox; he also obtained from Rome the approval to add to his title of Patriarch of Antioch that of Alexandria, and of Jerusalem.³ From that time on, there has been only one Catholic Melkite patriarch, who resides either at Damascus or in Cairo. The Orthodox have three distinct patriarchs; despite the small number of their faithful, they preserved their traditional rank in Orthodoxy: immediately

3. However, his predecessor, Theodosius VI, had already obtained the extension of his jurisdiction over the patriarchates of Alexandria and Jerusalem through a decree from the Sacred Congregation of Propaganda dated July 13, 1772.

following the ecumenical patriarch, and preceding the one from Moscow.

The Melkite community is the most ecumenical; the Orthodox are in communion with the vast Byzantine world and form a bridge between the Greek churches and the Slavonic churches. Of all oriental Catholics, the Melkites remained the most oriental; united to the Catholic world, they did not feel strange either to the Orthodox or to the Byzantine worlds. The influence of this church, which numbers some 400,000 Christians, emigrants included, far surpasses the local limits; it is very active in Syria, Lebanon, Jordan, Israel, and Egypt. Its emigrants have formed several parishes in France and in the various states of America, where the Orthodox also have bishoprics under the jurisdiction of the patriarchate of Antioch.

Nestorians and Chaldeans. The Nestorian church of Persia did not suffer at the hands of the Arabic government; it was always under pagan regime. During the war with the Persians, when the Abbassids ousted the Ommiads of Damascus and established the see of the calif of Bagdad (750), the Nestorian church found itself in a favorable position. The Catholics abandoned Seleucia and settled in Bagdad. Nestorians played an important role as officers of the court, as doctors, and as learned translators; their christological doctrine of the human personality of Christ was most closely related to Islamism. Mohammed himself had apparently been subjected to Nestorian influences.

The Nestorians however, soon enough lost their Christian settlements, implanted in Arabia along the Persian Gulf and absorbed by Islamism. They established new bishoprics in the West at Aleppo, Damascus, Jerusalem, and in Cyprus, and deployed an intense missionary activity in pagan lands on the eastern frontiers. Christian groups flourished and developed among the Turks, the Mongolians, the Chinese, and the Indians; from the eighth to the fourteenth century the Nestorian church was the leading Asiatic church. The Nestorians lost nothing by the arrival of the Seljuk Turks in Bagdad. Their fate was further improved by the Mongolian conquest of the thirteenth century, since Houlagou was the son of a Christian mother, and some Catholics of Mongolian origin attained the throne of Babylon. The West did not see fit, unfortunately, to accept the invitation extended by the Mongolians who were then friendly towards Christianity. When they became Moslems at the beginning of the fourteenth century, they pulled away from the Nestorians, and marked the decline of this church. Political troubles made the relations of Persia with China and Central Asia very difficult; as a result, Nestorian Christianity disappeared from Asia. The Mings destroyed the church in China, and the terrible invasion of Tamerlane ruined the Nestorian church of Persia. Those who escaped massacre and forced apostasy, fled to the mountainous regions along the lakes of Van and of Ourmia.

In the middle of the sixteenth century a move toward union with Rome began under the leadership of Patriarch Soulaqa. After various retractions a Catholic branch was set up and gained strength, which received the name of the Chaldean Church. Catholicism continued to develop, especially in the plains. The dissident Nestorians fled to the mountains of Kurdistan, where they formed a small political autonomy and called themselves Assyrians. Aroused against the Turks during the War of 1914–1918, and left to their sad fate by the Russians and the English, they were to leave their domain and flee to Iraq, where they suffered a horrible massacre in 1933; the Nestorian patriarch was subsequently self-exiled to Chicago in the United States. Several thousand Assyrians gathered in northern Djezir in Syrian territory; this isolation, and the prevailing hardships and poverty, reduced the Nestorian Church to a deplorable state. Approximately 120,000 were dispersed in Soviet territory, in the United States, and in the East; within their own territory, the members of this church now number only some 30,000 in Iraq and 20,000 in Iran. The Catholic branch, however, flourished. The Chaldeans number almost 200,000, of which 150,000 live in Iraq, where they constitute the most important Christian community of the country. Their patriarch, residing in Bagdad, was a member of the senate before the fall of the royal power in 1958.

The most brilliant jewel of the Chaldeo-Nestorian church is the Malabarese community of southern India. During the Middle Ages this community received its bishops from the Nestorian patriarch. When the Portuguese arrived, all the Christians favored union with Rome, but the Latinizing zeal of the Jesuits posed an obstacle to the establishment of a Catholic oriental hierarchy. In 1599 at the Synod of Diamper various Latinizing practices were imposed; to wit, the Malabarese were given a Latin Jesuit for bishop and were reunited to the archbishopric of Goa. These measures led to the schism of 1653; the dissident chief rejoined his group to the Monophysite-Jacobite patriarch of Antioch, whose titular had agreed to consecrate him bishop—the Chaldean Catholics of Babylon were inclined towards Catholicism at the time. The Italian Carmelites succeeded in bringing back most of the dissidents, but the Dutch occupation which have forced out Catholic missionaries stopped their work; they returned, however, about 1700. In the nineteenth century the Chaldean Catholic patriarch, Joseph Audo, attempted to include the Malabarese under his jurisdiction, and sent them a bishop. This action was not recognized by Rome. As a result, several thousand faithful followers of this bishop returned to the Nestorian schism.

In the Jacobite community, which sprang from the schism of 1653, a strong movement in favor of Catholicism has been in motion since 1930. Pius XI reestablished the Malabarese hierarchy independently of the Latins. This consisted of two ecclesiastical provinces: that of Ernakulam for the Malabarese of the traditional Chaldean rite, with 1,450,000 Christians, and the province of Trivandrum for those of the western Syriac rite, called the Syro-Malankerese, numbering some 80,000 Christians. Today, there remain only about 695,000 Jacobite Christians of the western Syrian rite, who follow the schism of 1653; some of these were influenced by Anglicanism. We can still account for 10,000 Nestorians, whose belief can be traced to the schism of the nineteenth century. The Malabarese community is full of life and vigor authentically rooted in Indian lands; it seems to be called to an important missionary role throughout the vast Indian territory.

The Syro-Jacobite Church. The Arab occupation assured the Jacobite Church its full legal recognition and even granted her favorable treatment with regard to the Melkite church, the only official one during the Byzantine Era. The Jacobite church was able to spread to Iraq, and her members took part in the development of Arabic culture, a role analogous to but less spectacular than that of the Nestorians. Internal divisions and the isolation experienced by the Jacobite community, starting with the thirteenth century, stopped the remarkable intellectual progress which had been so much in evidence up to that time. This com-

munity was certainly isolated, since it had at best very lax
canonical relations with the Copts alone, and it barely
supported efforts towards agreement with the Armenians.
In brief, despite the radical opposition to the christological
theses, the Jacobites were in contact only with Nestorians
because of their common Syriac culture. In the tenth century during the Byzantine occupation the untimely zeal of
the emperors in favor of conversions only served to deepen
this religious gap. During the Crusades, however, the
Jacobites appeared to be more conciliatory toward the
Latins, as a certain understanding existed between them.
The Jacobites were represented at the Council of Florence,
but all efforts of reunion failed.

When the Catholic movement grew stronger at Aleppo
in the seventeenth century upon the arrival of missionaries,
two Catholic patriarchs presided successively over the
Jacobite community from 1662 to 1702. The intrigues of
the heretics and of the Ottoman government prevented
the election of a Catholic successor and led to the persecution of Catholics. The Jacobite community split in two in
1783; this brought about the establishment of the Catholic
Syrian patriarchate, which preserved the early liturgical
tradition as the Jacobite patriarchate had done. The patriarchal sees, both Catholic and Monophysite, often changed
location; today, the Catholic patriarch resides in the monastery of Charfé, near Beirut, and the Orthodox patriarch
has recently relocated himself in Damascus.

Islamism severely punished the Jacobite community,
which now numbers only some 82,000 faithful; the Catholic patriarchate has 90,000. The Malabarese group which
joined the Jacobite church during the seventeenth century
numbers 695,000 dissidents and 80,000 Catholics. Her
ties with the Syrian patriarch are tenuous. This church,

rich in tradition, cannot survive without coming out of isolation and uniting itself to the other communities of the Antiochian patriarchate.

The Coptic Church. The Coptic church bore the fate of Christianity in Egypt because the Melkites for the most part had left the country with the Byzantine troops. Egypt had been protected from wars, invasions, and massacres, which had ravaged the Asiatic East. The decadence of the Coptic church somehow came about earlier than that of other communities as a result of continuous Moslem oppression, and of poverty and ignorance, to which both clergy and faithful fell victim. The cultured and Hellenized groups around Alexandria had left the country with the Byzantines and the mass of Copts was made up of enslaved peasants.

A certain intellectual renaissance flourished in the thirteenth and the fourteenth centuries, under the leadership of Abu-L-Barakat and Ibn Assal, but it was short lived. In the days of Mehemet Ali ignorance and misery had reduced the Coptic community to 100,000 throughout Egypt. But the liberalism of the founder of modern Egypt and the general sanitary measures that he promoted raised the number of Coptic faithful to nearly 2,000,000, which enabled them to hold their place in the direction of the country. This role was to become more important if the spiritual renaissance, now generated in the Coptic church, were to succeed in spreading among and penetrating within the masses. A small fraction of Copts became Catholic during the eighteenth century. The constitution of the Catholic Coptic patriarchate dates back only to 1899 and numbers about 75,000 faithful today.

The Coptic church's interest in Egypt stems from its numerical importance. It really represents itself as the

Egyptian national church since the other communities collectively represent only about one-eighth of the number of Copts, and their faithful are often of foreign origin, for example, Italian, Greek, and Syrian. For the Universal Church, the Copts, though not perpetuating the tradition of the Alexandrian Doctors, did at least keep the tradition of the Fathers of the Desert alive and gathered the vestiges of ancient Egyptian liturgy.

The church of Ethiopia was joined to the Coptic church, and, until recent years, has always been led by a single bishop chosen from Coptic monks by the patriarch of Alexandria. Ethiopia always enjoyed the advantage of being ruled by Christian kings; its evangelization was not profound, unfortunately, and the decadent Coptic church could not give this new church any real vitality. However, after a long, obscure period which followed the fall of the Axoum Dynasty, there was a renaissance during the thirteenth century under the Salomonide Dynasty; during the fifteenth century, King Zara Yakob led the country through its golden age. After him the leaders, pushed by Moslem menace, begged for help from the pope and from Portugal. This brought about the establishment of the first Jesuit mission (1536–1596). Strangely enough, this mission left no trace.

The first third of the seventeenth century witnessed the triumph of Catholicism in Ethiopia, as three leaders in succession declared themselves Catholic. The union was proclaimed in 1626, and Ethiopia received the Jesuit, Mendez, as patriarch. Strong methods employed to impose unity on the people, and the Latinizing practices of Mendez unleashed a civil war, which ended in a new break with Rome. Immediately missionaries were forbidden to enter the country; it was not until the nineteenth century that Ethiopia again welcomed their return.

The renaissance of Ethiopia under Menelik led the Ethiopian church to desire greater independence from the Coptic church. That is why Ethiopia received its first five national bishops besides a Coptic archbishop in 1929. When autonomy was declared during Italian occupation in 1937, it brought about a split between the two churches; but in 1941 the old status was re-established. In 1948 an agreement stipulated that the archbishop would be an Ethiopian and would have the power to consecrate his own bishops. In 1959 the head of the Ethiopian church received the title of patriarch-catholicos, which assured him autonomy as recognition of the spiritual and honorary primacy of the Coptic patriarch of Alexandria. Christian Ethiopia, which numbers eight million Monophysites and 120,000 Catholics, half of whom belong to the Ethiopian rite and the rest to the Latin rite, is called upon to play a dynamic role in Africa, but it is in need of strong spiritual assistance from the other churches.

The Armenian Church. The history of the Armenian people and that of the Armenian church are inseparable. Already the apple of discord between Romans and Persians, Armenia continued to be the same between Byzantines and Arabs. The Byzantines always tried to force Armenia to adhere to the Council of Chalcedon, and often brought pressure to bear upon her; a live antipathy thus set the Armenians against the Byzantines. The Arabs, on the other hand, masters of the country since 653, left to Armenia, political semifreedom and complete religious liberty. They placed a local Dynasty, the Pagratounis, at the head of the country.

In 1054 the Byzantines took over Armenia and attempted to impose unity by force. In 1071 the Seljuk Turks defeated the Byzantine troops and Armenia fell into the hands of the Turks. This marked the beginning of Armenian emigration, which led to a large settlement of Armenians in Syria and in Cilicia, where they founded the Kingdom of Lesser Armenia. The seat of the catholicosate moved to Romqala, near Edessa, then to Sis, capital of the Kingdom of Cilicia. The Armenians were in continuous, friendly contact with the crusaders of Antioch; the Armenian church became reunited with Rome and lived through a second golden age. But this union did not survive the fall of the Cilician Kingdom of 1375 under the blows of the Mameluk sultans of Cairo. At this time the Armenian church split up into several autonomous jurisdictions and the supreme see again returned to Greater Armenia at Etchmiadzin.

At the outset of the seventeenth century, the Persians under Shah Abbas vanquished the Ottomans, who had been masters of the country since the fifteenth century. The Persians imposed such unbearable rule on a large part of Armenia, that many Christians were forced to embrace Islamism. In 1826, however, a portion of this Armenia became part of the empire of the czars. The Armenians preserved their personality despite all the continuous divisions and vexations of Ottoman, Russian, and Persian rulers. At the end of the nineteenth century and the beginning of the twentieth they suffered systematic massacres at the instigation of Sultan Abdulhamid (1894–95, 1909) or at the hands of the generals known as the Young Turks (1915–1920). After that date, there were no more Armenians in Turkey except for Constantinople.

The New Armenian Republic, founded in 1918, fell

into the hands of the Soviets, in whose territory the supreme catholicos now resides under the title of Etchmadzine. The Armenians of the diaspora are under the jurisdiction of the titular catholicos of Sis, a refugee at Antelias in Lebanon since 1921—the French evacuated Cilicia after they had occupied it in 1918—and are ruled by patriarchs established in Jerusalem and Constantinople. Soviet propaganda lured several thousand Armenians into the Soviet Republic, but they do not seem to have found the anticipated paradise. The Armenians, who now number nearly 2,500,000, of whom 2,000,000 are in Soviet Armenia, always dream of reestablishing their country.

The Catholic Armenians. Catholic tendencies did not disappear after the Crusades; consequently we find Armenians at the Council of Florence. In 1740 the Armenian bishop of Aleppo, a genuine Catholic, was elected catholicos; he organized the Catholic Armenian patriarchate despite the opposition of the Turks; his jurisdiction covered Cilicia, Syria, Mesopotamia, and Egypt. The rest of the Catholic Armenians were under the jurisdiction of the apostolic vicar of Constantinople; Pius VIII gave them a primate archbishop, and the two jurisdictions were fused in 1867. The center of the patriarchate, today, is in Lebanon. There are now about 180,000 Catholic Armenians.

The Maronites. The Maronite church disappeared to the mountains of Lebanon and remained sheltered from Moslem oppression; it existed in a state of semifreedom and developed without hindrance. Hence, in the Modern Era, it acquired an importance beyond the merits of its feeble origin.

Nothing definite is known of the history of the Maronites before the Crusades. William of Tyre, who reported their union with Rome, estimated that they numbered

40,000. They were joined with the Crusaders and became part of the Frankish bourgeoisie, a position which was strengthened by their pro-Western sympathies. In the seventeenth century, one of their own was named French consul at Beirut, and Louis XIV considered them to be part of the French nation.

Relations with Rome, interrupted during the Mameluk period, were reestablished at the beginning of the sixteenth century. The Maronites were strongly influenced by the Latins in their liturgy and discipline; many were trained in Rome, where Gregory XIII had founded a Maronite college for them, and some became brilliant orientalists, such as the Assemani. At the start of the sixteenth century, Lebanon welcomed western civilization under the leadership of Fakhreddine, the great Druse emir. The Maronites did not take a back seat, and the present-day modern structures date back to the days of this Islamo-Christian collaboration. After the massacres of 1860 Lebanon was ruled by Christian governors until 1915. Today, the president of the republic is traditionally a Maronite, and the Maronite patriarch enjoys a considerable politico-religious prestige, even in the eyes of the non-Christians.

The Maronite Church, which numbers in the East and in the diaspora nearly 800,000 faithful, has great religious potential and easily lends itself to its ecumenical and missionary vocation. The liturgical reform now underway, which is expected to restore the Maronite rite in its primitive Syrian purity and to adapt it to new circumstances, should greatly assist the Maronite community to realize its mission.

CHAPTER VI · THE CHURCH IN THE BYZANTINE WORLD

THE PATRIARCHATE OF CONSTANTINOPLE

THE BYZANTINE EMPIRE prolonged the Roman world until the end of the Middle Ages. There was nothing in her that would insure continuity, nothing that would permit a transition from antiquity to the Modern Era, without pain or rupture. However, because the West and the eastern Semitic provinces fell into the hands of the Germans or the Arabs, the Byzantine Empire was reduced to Greek-speaking provinces, and even to a single patriarchate of Constantinople which was expanded in 732 to include the Balkan regions, previously dependent on Rome. The results were a certain narrowness of outlook and a lack of intelligence with respect to other traditions, which caused a stiffening of relations with separated Eastern churches, especially with the Armenians and Jacobites who were in direct contact with the empire. Pressures were brought to bear on the Orthodox Melkite churches weakened by Islamism, and gradually contact with Rome was weakened, because it was bound more and more to the barbarian world, where primacy and customs were less and less honored.

Taken by itself, this narrowing led to the coinciding of Orthodoxy with the church of Byzantium whose head took the title of ecumenical patriarch. Nothing very new happened in the Byzantine church after the victory of Orthodoxy over the Iconoclasts (787–843), except for the evangelization of the Slavonic world and the appearance of palamasian theology.

During the ninth century, the Byzantine church seems to have attained, in its internal structures, a perfection which sheltered her from the marks of history. It seemed to have been cut off from the world, and to have been more concerned with avoiding the world than with sanctifying it in order to go beyond it and to lead it to a celestial life through asceticism and contemplation. Christian humanism seems to have been unknown in Byzantium, because the sacred existed with the pagan, but did not try to Christianize it. Solitary, monastic life predominated; the liturgies, celebrated in all their pageantry, were more celestial than terrestrial; sacred art was developed for the benefit of worship, but there was neither philosophy, nor literature, nor profane art inspired by Christianity. Similarly, charitable works or Christian social action were practically unknown; the emperors themselves, who wanted to be looked upon as pontiffs, did not live as truly Christian princes.

Disengaged from any temporal plan, the church also did not experience any veritable progress in dogma, as was the case in the West, nor did she come up with any new forms of holiness or of religious life. The history of the Byzantine church was to be a particularly external history of expansion or withdrawal of the political power of Constantinople. Contact, today, with the West through emigration, through cultural exchanges or ecumenical movements, or through the Communist regime, which is a fruit of western thought, is posing a new problem for the Orthodox church and is leading it into a crisis of growth.

The Macedonian Dynasty (867–1057) spread the Byzantine hierarchy in the rhythm of its conquests in the West in southern Italy, and Bulgaria, and in the East in northern Syria and northern Armenia. But early in the eleventh century the Normans recaptured southern Italy and advanced into Asia Minor, leaving only a small band to the West.

Christianity would henceforth be reduced to a minority religion in Asia Minor and would be liquidated by the Republic of Mustapha Kemal. The Serbian and Bulgarian Kingdoms were reformed in the West, where the hardest blow was struck by the Latins of the Fourth Crusade, who conquered Constantinople and Greece in 1204, and installed their hierarchy. The Greek patriarch of Constantinople left his see and fled to Nicea; as a result, the gap which already separated the Greeks from the Latins was broadened further.

The Greeks regained Constantinople in 1261, at which time the empire, led by Michael Paleologus, did not enjoy the power and prestige it had previously known. The emperors attempted in vain to restore religious unity with the West to avoid a return of the Latins who would weaken them in their fight against the Ottomans. After rising slightly during the fourteenth century under Palamas and Cabasilas, Byzantium fell into the hands of the Turks in 1453.

All attempts at unity were frustrated. Theological life was reduced drastically, to be taken up in the nineteenth century; although there were some apostasies, the majority remained Christian. The sultans kept the patriarchal function, but the designation of new patriarchs came under their jurisdiction, and the position was often offered to the highest bidder. The patriarchs, frequently deposed, would often be returned and reinstalled on their thrones. Despite humiliations and restrictions brought on by the Ottoman occupation, the prestige of the patriarchs increased in Constantinople, which once again became the see of an empire equal in size to the pre-Arab oriental empire. The jurisdiction of the ecumenical patriarch quickly spread to all the Orthodox of the Ottoman Empire to such a degree that in the eighteenth century the Greeks of Constantinople rid themselves of all the important sees of the Orthodox except those in Russia.

The reawakening of nationalities in the Ottoman Empire during the nineteenth century brought about the formation of the Balkan states. Political independence—the Sultan's power was weakened—was accompanied by a religious independence of the ecumenical patriarchate. The latter spent many unhappy hours as a result of the Greek-Turkish war of 1922. He was almost compelled to leave the Turkish territory with the majority of the Greek population, but the Lausanne Accords of 1923 set up the preservation of the rights of the ecumenical patriarch at Istanbul.

Today, the patriarchate of Constantinople has jurisdiction only over the Orthodox of the Turkish Republic, certain Greek islands, and over the Orthodox living in western Europe and in America—at least, over those who speak Greek—because the Orthodox born of other nationalities want to depend on their own national communities. Hence, within the same western region, the Orthodox belong to different jurisdictions according to their national origin; this poses a grave problem for Orthodox ecclesiology, because it no longer has a single, clear direction. The patriarch of Constantinople has merely a primacy of honor, and the initial primacy which is his by law, is exercised over the Slavonic as well as Arabic world by the patriarch of Moscow.

THE CHURCHES DERIVED FROM THE
PATRIARCHATE OF CONSTANTINOPLE

The Bulgarian Church. In 864 Christianity found its way into Bulgaria with the conversion of Prince Boris, who hesitated for a while between Constantinople and Rome. On this occasion, a conflict for power was being waged between the leading sees which inflamed the quarrel of Photius with Pope Nicholas I. When the disciples of St. Cyril and St. Methodius were driven out of Moravia, Boris welcomed them. They took up the leadership of the Bulgarian church and translated the Byzantine liturgy into Slavonic, the old Bulgarian of the ninth century. This translation later spread to the other Slavonic churches.

When the Bulgarians strengthened their authority, they demanded that their prince be given the title of Czar, and that their archbishop be given the title of patriarch. When Constantinople refused to give these titles, they turned to Rome where in 927 they were given both the crown and the patriarchate. But the Byzantine Emperor, Basil II, crushed the Bulgarians in 1018, and annexed their empire whose patriarch had for some time held the title of Archbishop of Achrida.

At the end of the twelfth century the Bulgarians regained their independence and gave themselves a patriarch at Tirnovo, whose title was recognized by Innocent III. This patriarchate lasted until 1393, at which date

Bulgaria fell into the hands of the Ottomans; the see of Achrida then became a patriarchate, but disappeared in 1767. Bulgaria was annexed as a simple territory to the patriarchate of Constantinople, and fell under the exclusive domination of the Greeks, who tried to destroy every trace of Slavonic in it.

In the nineteenth century the national conscience was aroused, and the Bulgarians wanted to rid themselves of the Greeks and the Turks, with the help of Russia. They demanded an autonomous hierarchy, but were refused; whereupon they declared their independence in 1872. Their archbishop, who took the title of Exarch, their chiefs and all the people were excommunicated as schismatics by the ecumenical patriarch. The Greeks, enemies of the Bulgarians, were the only ones to enforce this decision. Religious autonomy was strengthened by the formation of the Bulgarian state, and relations with the ecumenical patriarch were reestablished in 1945, when the Bulgarian church and its self-appointed head were officially recognized. A few years later in 1953 the patriarchate was reestablished, but Constantinople did not recognize it until 1961, since the declaration of 1953 had been made without her consultation.

Let us point out, finally, that in 1860 an important move of reunion with Rome was underway while the Bulgarians sought their independence from the Greeks of Constantinople, but this was quickly thwarted and averted by the Russians. The Catholics of the Byzantine rite in Bulgaria today number about 6,000.

The Serbian Church. The Serbs settled in the Balkans during the seventh century, and have been split ever since their evangelization between the Roman and the Byzantine rites. They were annexed in 983 by the Bulgarian

Empire, then taken with Bulgaria into the Byzantine Empire in 1018; hence they were under complete Byzantine influence. At the end of the twelfth century Stephan Némanya reestablished national independence. At that time the Serbs were in communion with Rome, but after the fall of the Latin Empire in Constantinople, they withdrew from the Roman see. In the fourteenth century Etienne Douchan brought the kingdom to its peak. In wanting to play the part of emperor, he had the metropolitan of Ipek consecrated as patriarch, and he in turn crowned him emperor. The Serbian Empire was broken, however, in 1389 by the Ottomans at Kossovo. In 1459 Mohammed II suppressed the patriarchate of Ipek and reassigned Serbia to the Greco-Bulgarian archbishopric of Achrida. Almost a hundred years later in 1557 the Great Vizier, Sokoli, obtained the restoration of the patriarchate of Ipek, as a favor from his brother.

In 1690, to avoid the repraisals of the Turks, after their defeat in Vienna, 37,000 Serbian families fled to the Austro-Hungarian Empire under the leadership of the patriarch to avoid the repraisals of the Turks; a semi-autonomous metropolis was set up at Karlowitz in the Austrian Empire because of the ever-rising number of refugees. In 1766 during the suppression of the patriarchate of Ipek by the Turks, which was directly reassigned to Constantinople, the Serbian refugees in Austria-Hungary took advantage of this to give the title of patriarch to the metropolitan of Karlowitz.

The Serbs of the Ottoman Empire obtained their political autonomy in 1830 only after costly fighting. The Serbian church was given its independence from the ecumenical patriarch, provided that the metropolitan of Belgrade, freely chosen by her, would be confirmed and invested by Constantinople, and provided that he would be paid an annual tribute by her. In 1878 after the Congress of Berlin Serbia broke all vassal ties, both political and religious, with Constantinople.

In 1918 following the Balkan War (1912–1913) and the defeat of the Turks and Austrians, the state of Yugoslavia was established by successive union with Serbia of Slavonia, with Croatia, and with Bosnia and Herzegovina, separated either from the Austro-Hungarian Empire, or from independent Montenegro, or from Macedonia, formerly Ottoman, but claimed at the same time by the Bulgarians and the Greeks. On November 12, 1920, the patriarchate was restored, and the titular took the title of archbishop of Ipek, metropolitan of Belgrade and Karlowitz, and patriarch of the Serbs.

Yugoslavia has slightly more than 7,000,000 Orthodox, nearly 6,000,000 Catholics of the Latin rite, the majority of which are Croatian and Slavonic, and 2,200,000 Moslems, principally in Bosnia and Herzegovina. The Catholics of Byzantine rite are grouped under the jurisdiction of the Bishop of Kryvetsi, and they number about 55,000.

The Church of Rumania. The regions of present-day Rumania were colonized by the Romans and quickly evangelized by them. At the time of the invasions of the Middle Ages these territories fell into the hands either of the Bulgarian Empire comprising the principalities of Moldavia and Wallachia, or of the Hungarian Kingdom, which then possessed Transylvania. During Byzantine domination, they were attracted by the Bulgarian supremacy, and for a long time were under the jurisdiction of the Greco-Bulgarian archbishop of Achrida. The Ottoman conquest allowed a certain autonomy to the Moldavian principalities, but they were subjected to Greek influence, especially in the eighteenth century, and were subject to the ecumenical patriarch.

Transylvania escaped the grasp of the Turks and remained in the hands of the Hungarians until 1688, when it was rejoined to the Austrian Empire of the Hapsburgs. The Rumanian Byzantine church of Transylvania joined Rome at the Synod of Alba-Julia in 1697. The Rumanian Orthodox who refused this union were without hierarchy; they were first under the jurisdiction of the Serbian Metropolitan of Karlowitz, residing in the Austrian Empire, and later received their own metropolitan in 1864. Bukovina, an integral part of Moldavia which had received its own metropolitan in 1873, was rejoined to Austria during the following year.

The Rumania of today was established by emancipation, at the Congress of Paris in 1856, from two principalities of Moldavia and Wallachia, and by their union under the authority of Alexander Cuza. Political independence encouraged religious independence, and after long evasions the patriarchate of Constantinople recognized the Independent Rumanian Church in 1885.

After the War of 1914–1918 the Kingdom of Rumania expanded at the expense of Austria, of Transylvania, and of Bukovina; it rejoined Bessarabia which was taken from the Russians who later recovered it at the end of World War II. Immediately it became necessary to unite all of its elements. On February 25, 1925, the metropolitan primate of Wallachia was proclaimed patriarch of all of Rumania. The organization of Catholic bishops was regulated in 1927 by a concordat with the Holy See. The Uniates, or Catholics of Eastern rite, have a metropolitan entitled Faragas-Alba-Julia, who resides at Blaj, and five

suffragan bishoprics. The Communist government of today has officially suppressed the Uniate church and has
rejoined her to the Orthodox church.

The Russian Church. The most beautiful jewel of Constantinople is the Russian church. Christianity came into
Russia during the ninth century through a combination of
Byzantine-Bulgarian and western influences. It was officially established with the baptism of Vladimir, Prince of
Kiev, in 987, who married the sister of Basil II, Emperor
of Byzantium. The Byzantine-Slavonic rite was imposed
from the start of the eleventh century. In 1307 the metropolitan see of Kiev was established, and most of its titulars
were Greeks sent by Constantinople. During this same
century the monastic holiness of Athos spread, and Russia
then experienced the form of a new spiritual *élan.* This
advance and the friendly relations with the West were
broken in 1240 by the Mongol invasion, which began an
oppression in Russia that lasted two centuries.

The metropolitans of Kiev abandoned the destroyed capital and resided at Vladimir and then at Moscow. From
1325 each bore the respective title of metropolitan of Kiev
and metropolitan of Moscow. The political and religious
preeminence of Moscow, previously known as an insignificant city, dates back to this period. Politically, Moscow was to rebuild the national unity around itself and
expel the Mongols. We note here that Moscow is located
in a region which had never been in touch with the West;
therefore, the dislocation of the political and dynamic center of Russia from Kiev to Moscow would weigh heavily
on the relations with Rome.

While Russia was still broken up into several principalities at the beginning of the fourteenth century, two states,
Poland and Lithuania, developed on its western frontier.

These united in 1386 under the rule of the Jagellons. Officially of the Latin rite, these princes incorporated into their state vast territories of Byzantine rite, such as Galicia, Volhynia, and the Ukraine with Kiev. In the Polish-Lithuanian state, those of Byzantine rite did not have the same civil rights as did the Latins, an inequality which was the source of discord between the two churches; the Byzantines remained loyal to the metropolitan of Kiev-Moscow who resided in Moscow.

In 1441 the Metropolitan of Kiev, Isidore, returned from the Council of Florence, where he had greatly championed union with Rome. He proclaimed union in the various churches of the Ukraine, but, once in Moscow, he was taken prisoner by Prince Basil, who adhered to Orthodoxy. Isidore succeeded in escaping, but since he had been poorly received in Lithuania, he fled to Rome. He was replaced in Moscow by metropolitan Jonas, whose jurisdiction over the Byzantines of Poland and Lithuania was recognized by the Jagellons. In 1459, however, Rome assigned a Bulgarian by the name of Gregory to the see of Kiev, who was accepted by Poland and even recognized by Constantinople. (Isidore had meanwhile been given charge of Constantinople.) The Metropolitan, Jonas of Moscow, at the same time lost his jurisdiction over the Polish-Lithuanians; this marked the definitive parting of the two sees of Kiev and Moscow. From this point on, we shall treat separately the Russian church of Moscow which is fiercely anti-Roman, and the Ukrainian church of Russia or Ruthenian church which is more friendly to Rome and to the West.

The Muscovite Russian Church. Since the patriarchate of Constantinople had escaped the union of Florence and had come under Turkish domination, Moscow, now powerful, considered itself in the fifteenth century as heir to the Byzantine Empire, and guardian of Orthodoxy. She, therefore, no longer wanted to depend on Constantinople. The metropolitans were chosen from Russian clergy by the grand prince; Moscow was even referred to as a third Rome.

In the sixteenth century Ivan IV was crowned Czar, and was considered to be the political leader of all the Orthodox. The sovereignty of the Russian church was definitely established in 1589 by the institution of the patriarchate of Moscow, which was given fifth rank after the four oriental sees. In the seventeenth century the reforms of Patriarch, Nikon (1652–1666) which attempted to unify Russian and Greek customs brought about the schism of the old vanguard believers (who, today, number nearly eighteen million).

Peter the Great wanted to utilize the church to realize his domestic policies; he, therefore, suppressed the patriarchate in 1720, and replaced it with a supreme synod, presided over by a member of the government, the procurator. The czar thus became the actual head of the church. In the nineteenth century a theological renewal came to life under the leadership of Nicholas I, who embodied authoritarianism and identified Russia with Orthodoxy. But it was impossible to promote progress of ideas by force. The Revolution of 1905 set the stage for that of 1917 which brought the czars into the turmoil. The Russian Council, reunited after the fall of Nicholas II, re-established the patriarchate in the person of Tykhon, metropolitan of Moscow, who soon found himself confronted with an atheistic Communist regime which he courageously opposed. He was stopped in 1922, deposed in 1923, and was not replaced.

The persecuted church was torn between the choices of attitudes she should take toward the government.

In 1943 the incontestable patriotism of the Christians during the war drew a certain tolerance from Stalin for them. Sergius, Metropolitan of Moscow, was allowed to take the title of patriarch; his successor, Alexis, elected in 1945, tried to revive the Russian, pre-Czarist tradition and to spread his influence over the Slavonic countries. The rapid renewal of the Russian church since 1945 bespeaks a vitality and a faith worthy of all esteem. Despite the dearth of religious propaganda in recent years, the Russian church lends itself well to the ecumenical current. Russian emigrants are spread out into several jurisdictions, and their massive arrival in the West after the revolution had some worthwhile effects, such as a better mutual understanding and an enrichment of Orthodox theology.

The Ukrainian Church. Gregory, the metropolitan sent by Rome in 1459, strengthened the union of Florence; the Ukrainian hierarchy was in communion with Rome and Constantinople despite the split between these two sees. This abnormal situation could not long endure. About 1520 the union established in Florence was rejected, and a little later the Protestant influence spread throughout the country. The ministry of the Jesuits, Skarga and Possevino, prepared the way for a new union. At a synod held in 1590, a decision was made to break with the oriental patriarchs, and in 1595 union with Rome was proclaimed at Brest. Among the conditions stipulated were the following: maintenance of the rites and bishoprics and protection against the ecumenical patriarch. Two bishops out of eight withheld their signatures; they joined the Protestants to fight the union. Elsewhere, the Polish-Latins did not support the Byzantine Catholics and refused them the privileges accorded to the Latins.

In 1620 the patriarch of Jerusalem, when travelling in the Ukraine, consecrated six Orthodox bishops; the Orthodox hierarchy was thus established and was recognized by the government. From then on, Kiev had two metropolitans. St. Josaphat, Bishop of Polock, was assassinated and died a martyr for having been the ardent supporter of unity. In 1667 in the Treaty of Andrusovo, the Ukraine ceded her eastern part to Moscovite Russia. Kiev was henceforth lost to Catholic Christians, but she had planted the seed of oriental theological influence in Russia. Unity had gained much ground in the Ukraine under Polish rule. In fact, the number of its Byzantine Catholics in the seventeenth century was estimated at several million. However, the splitting up of Poland at the end of the eighteenth century in 1772, 1793, and 1795, separated the Catholic Ukraine into two parts; the one fell to Russia, the other to Austria in Galicia.

Practically speaking, the Russians revoked unity and forcibly incorporated the Catholic Ukrainians into the National Orthodox church. The Uniate members were later suppressed in 1839 by Nicholas I; the only diocese which remained was the diocese of Chelm which was also abolished in 1875. Freedom of conscience was proclaimed in 1905, whereupon several hundred thousand Ukrainians hastened to embrace Catholicism, choosing the Latin rite, because the Uniate Byzantine church was not allowed. The Uniate Church did, nonetheless, come to life in embryo form. The Russian intellectual Soloviëv contributed to this renewal, and Pius X welcomed its converts openly. Unfortunately, the War and the Revolution of 1917 put an end to this revival. The Ukraine worked in vain in 1917 and again in 1942 to separate itself from Muscovite Russia, but a portion of the western Ukraine fell to Poland, which had been resurrected in 1918.

The Ruthenians who had established themselves within Austria were respected there, but after the defeat of 1918, most of them came under the authority of Poland, the rest under Czechoslovakia. In Poland, the Uniates were again harassed by the Latins. In 1944, because of the dislocation of the Soviet frontiers, the Ruthenians of Galicia found themselves under Soviet rule. They acted as they had done under the Czarist government. As a result, the Uniate church was officially rejoined to the patriarchate of Moscow and their bishops were imprisoned. In Czechoslovakia, also, the Uniate bishops were arrested; the Christians secretly remained faithful to their beliefs, while awaiting better days. However, the Ruthenian emigration towards Western Europe and North America was sufficient to justify an independent organization. The Catholic Ruthenians in Canada have their hierarchy, as do those in western Europe and in the United States, but the Orthodox Ukrainians have separated themselves from their Russian brethren who were of the same belief.

The Church of Greece. The church of Greece is the only Orthodox church which still represents an independent majority; the others live today under Communist domination, under Moslem rule, or under western influence. Consequently, the church of Greece is of dynamic importance for the ecumenical dialogue. Furthermore, she remains the most faithful to the patriarchate of Constantinople, to which she is linked by virtue of her history, her race and her language. The church of Greece had left the patriarchate of Constantinople in 1830 at the time of its national independence, only because Constantinople was under Ottoman domination. It expanded as soon as the national territory became larger at the expense of the ecumenical patriarch; and, in 1923 it acquired all the refugees from Asia Minor. A transfer of population had been stipulated by treaties. Among those transferred, a small group of Catholics of the Byzantine rite, formed in Constantinople in 1860, settled in Athens, and have been under the jurisdiction of an apostolic bishop-exarch since 1911.

Since World War II the Greek church has demonstrated a pertinent theological and pastoral vitality. It is participating actively in the ecumenical movement, and a missionary interest is beginning to develop. The laity has played an important role in the spiritual redirection of this church in a movement known as "Zoe Apostoliki Diakonia."

Small National Churches. Outside of the large national churches, the Orthodox, following the principle of nationality, founded some small independent churches in countries where they were in the minority, such as the Orthodox church of Finland, the Orthodox church of Poland, the Orthodox church of Czechoslovakia and the Orthodox church of Albania. The Albanians who escaped into southern Italy during the Ottoman conquests formed, together with inhabitants of Greek origin who had settled there since the Byzantine occupation, a Catholic community of Byzantine rite, called the Italo-Greeks. They have their own hierarchy at Lungro and their cultural center at the monastery of Grotta Ferrara.

There are also two small national churches separated from the patriarchate of Antioch, which now belong to the Greco-Slavonic world: first, the church of Cyprus, whose autonomy in relation to Antioch had been decided at the Council of Ephesus in 431; second, the church of

Georgia, subjected to the Russian church after that country was rejoined to the Russian empire of the czars in the eighteenth century. In 1917 the Georgian church recovered its autonomy and elected its archbishop, who has the title of catholicos.

THE SITUATION OF THE ORIENTAL
CHURCHES TODAY

After these thirteen centuries of history the church of the Orient remained true to itself although its effectiveness diminished considerably in Africa and Asia. It did, however, develop in eastern Europe, and its external appearance was thereby modified.

The Oriental church is still divided into six different rites: the Byzantine, the Coptic, the Armenian, the Chaldean, the Maronite, and the Syriac. Numerically, the Byzantine rite is more important than all the others. There are 175,000,000 eastern faithful, if we estimate the Christians in the Union of Soviet Socialist Republics to be approximately 115,000,000. Of the remaining, five non-Byzantine rites collectively number only 16,000,000 Christians; 8,000,000 of these are in Ethiopia.

From a dogmatic point of view orientals can be divided into the following three groups.

A. Churches born as result of opposition to fifth-century Councils.

While Monothelitism completely disappeared, and Nestorianism was significantly weakened—numbering at present 120,000 spread far and wide—the Monophysite churches still have a sufficiently important number of followers, approximately 13,500,000 spread out in these three autonomous communities of different rites:

The Coptic community, patriarchate of Constantinople, of Coptic rite with her daughter, the church of Ethiopia, of Ethiopian rite.

The Syrian-Jacobite community, patriarchate of Antioch, with the Jacobite group of southern India, of Syrian rite.

The Armenian community, of Armenian rite, divided into several jurisdictions.

The Copts are in full communion with the Jacobites, but the Armenians have their own particular theological color.

B. The Orthodox church, faithful to the first seven councils.

Numerically, this Church represents the most important block of 151,000,000 people. It refused the dogmatic advances later realized in the West and opposed the strengthening of papal authority during the Middle Ages; hence the reason for its break with Rome. Finally, religious sensibility and psychology, rather than dogmatic concepts separate these two gatherings of Christians from one another.

The Orthodox have all been of Byzantine rite, since the Melkites and the Georgians had aligned themselves with Constantinople; but their liturgical languages differ. They form a unique community, attracted by the two different poles of the Greek spirit of Constantinople and the Russian soul of Moscow.

Ecclesiastically and juridically, Orthodoxy lacks a center of permanent unity since its supreme authority is the ecumenical council. The following is a list of churches which today constitutes the Orthodox communion, and the number of faithful belonging to each one:

1. The patriarchate of Constantinople whose jurisdiction covers Turkey, 105,000, the Dodecanese, 102,000. Mt. Athos, the autonomous metropolis of Crete, 450,000 and the archbishopric of central and western Europe, 70,000.

2. The patriarchate of Alexandria, which spreads its jurisdiction over Africa, 150,000.

3. The patriarchate of Antioch, which covers nineteen archbishoprics in Syria and Lebanon, and four in America, 500,000.

4. The patriarchate of Jerusalem, in Israel and in Jordan, 45,000.

5. The patriarchate of Moscow, 115,000,000 (?), Christians on whom depend the Orthodox churches of China, 5,000, of Korea, 1,000, and of Japan, 75,000. Russian emigrants are spread out in several jurisdictions.

6. The patriarchate of Serbia, four metropolitans and seventeen bishoprics, 7,000,000.

7. The patriarchate of Bulgaria, eleven metropolitans, 6,000,000.

8. The patriarchate of Rumania, five metropolitans and five bishoprics, 12,000,000.

9. The catholicosate of Tiflis (Tbilisi in Georgia), 2,000,000.

10. The church of Greece, 67 metropolitans, 7,000,000.

11. The independent church of Poland, 350,000.

12. The independent church of Czechoslovakia 200,000.

13. The archbishopric of Finland, 70,000.

14. The archbishopric of Cyprus, 400,000.

15. The church of Albania, 160,000.

16. The archbishopric of Sinai, which covers the monastery and its associates, 100.

The Orthodox now feel the need for greater unity, the first manifestation of which is reflected in recent congresses held at Rhodes at the request of His Holiness Athenagoras, Ecumenical Patriarch.

C. Oriental Catholics.

These comprise approximately 10,500,000 faithful who entered into communion with Rome at different dates, but who preserved, for the most part, their liturgical and disciplinary traditions. They came from a background of either old christological heresies or from Byzantine Orthodoxy. Certain communities were perhaps never separated from Rome, but lived apart because of political circumstances. All of the present-day Catholic communities have arisen because they have recognized the dogmatic progress alive in the West. This recognition has constituted an abrupt change for them and a break in communion with the rest of the Orient, except for the Italo-Greeks in Italy.

Only the Maronite community has always adhered completely to unity. For the others, unity was merely partial and occasioned an internal split and a duplication of Catholic hierarchy for the Catholic faithful. Most of the time it was the traditional hierarchy who brought about a partial or total unity, while the Orthodox hierarchy would later re-establish itself with the support of other Orthodox churches and the Ottoman government. Occasionally Rome would set up a Catholic hierarchy for the Catholic faithful of a given area.

Catholic Orientals are called Uniates by the Orthodox. This is an unofficial term which carries pejorative connotations when used by them.

The following is a list of the various groups of eastern Catholics:

I. Byzantine Rite Groups
>   Ukrainians: in Galicia, Czechoslovakia, North
>   America, and western Europe, nearly 5,500,000.
>   Rumanians: 1,563,000[1]
>   Melkites: 400,000
>   Greeks: 6,000
>   Yugoslavs: 55,000
>   Italo-Greeks: 75,000
>   Bulgarians: 6,000
>   The Hungarian diocese of Hajdudorog: 195,000

II. Syriac Language Groups
>   Maronites: 800,000
>   Malabarese: 1,450,000
>   Malankarese: 80,000
>   Chaldeans: 200,000
>   Syriacs: 90,000

III. Armenian Rite: 180,000

IV. Coptic Rite:
>   The patriarchate of Alexandria: 90,000
>   Ethiopia: 60,000

These groups are not unified among themselves according to an eastern plan; they are linked together by Rome, where The Congregation for Oriental Churches, founded in 1917 by Pope Benedict XI, replaces for them the ensemble of Roman congregations. Before then, they depended on the Sacred Congregation of Propaganda. The new code of canon law for the oriental churches, which is about to appear, will insure this unity still further yet it will allow for various particularities of discipline.

From a political viewpoint the oriental churches live under various regimes. Approximately 148,000,000, or 85 per cent of oriental Christians are ruled by a Communist

1. The figures given are those prior to the steps taken to assimilation after World War II.

regime. Among them, 6,000,000 are Catholic but are constrained—we cannot tell to what extent—to enter the Orthodox church. The Communist regime is more tolerant toward Orthodox and even Latins, than it is toward Byzantine Catholics.

In Islamic territories of the Near East there are 5,000,-000 Oriental Christians, among whom we count today 1,146,000 Catholics; Christians now make up a feeble minority, as they are only 5 per cent of the total population. The Christian community is practically extinct in Afghanistan and Arabia. In Iran, they amount to only 0.76 per cent of the population, and in Turkey only 0.8 per cent since the massacres and transfer of population of 1915–1923. In Iraq we find about 4 per cent of the population to be Christian, in Jordan only 10 per cent. In the United Arab Republic, as in Syria, the Christians represent about 13.5 per cent of the inhabitants. Lebanon is the only country in the Near East where Christians form a slight majority. Among these Christians, Catholics are the more numerous owing to the Maronite community.

Outside of these two zones, within the free world there are also nearly 22,000,000 eastern Christians, of whom about 3,000,000 are Catholics. In this group the church of Greece with 7,000,000 Christians is the most important. The church of Ethiopia with 8,000,000 is next in importance then the Malabarese of southern India with 2,000,000. Finally, almost 5,000,000 Christians are dispersed through western Europe and North and South America. The church of Greece and the emigrated orientals live in the Western political world. Consequently, they stand at the forefront of ecumenism.

PART II · EAST AND WEST

IT IS DIFFICULT to establish the precise moment when the two Christian worlds, East and West, became two well-defined entities. In pressing for such a date one risks oversimplification at the expense of truth. However, it is an indisputable fact, that ever since the peace of Constantine, we find ourselves confronted with two distinct divisions within Christianity. They had been founded to converse with one another and to be the source of the multiple rebirths of the Church in the various cultures. Regrettably, each isolated itself from the other, thus making their complementarity inoperative. Finally, they reached a parting of the ways.

Many attempts to mend the torn robe of Christ did not succeed, and thus we find ourselves in a sad state of separation, harmful to all. We shall rapidly look at the history of the relations between East and West to try to extract the cause and the meaning of this breaking apart. Then, we shall examine the attitude to be adopted in face of this separation; finally, we shall study the authentic relations which should prevail between the two parts of Christianity.

DIVERSITY WITHIN UNITY

DURING THE FIRST three centuries the Church was like a fraternity of churches among which Rome maintained unity and set the pattern. The same diversity was evident, both in the East and in the West; the clandestine life of the often-persecuted Christians lent itself to such a regime. The pagan emperor did not intervene in the internal affairs of Christian communities.

Once the empire became Christian, it was necessary to organize the Church on the universal plan of the *Oikoumene*. In the East since the time of Constantine, the emperor took it upon himself to insure the unity and universality of the Church. To implement this he convened bishops to ecumenical councils, the decisions of which became the law of the empire.

In Rome, where the popes always conceived the Universal Church to be centered in their primacy, the supreme emphasis was apostolic; when they went to the councils, they arrived with prepared formulas. In the East the primary source of law was the canon of the council, whereas in Rome, it was the decree of the pope. These divergent views are at the very root of the conflicts which before the great schism so often set Rome against Constantinople. During the period which extends from 337 to 843, the religious politics of the emperor provoked 217 years of misunderstanding between the two sees.   .

Certainly, the East recognized Roman primacy, but it did not understand this principle in the same way as Rome did. Constantinople admitted the pope's right of intervention in doctrinal questions to safeguard the purity of tradition, but she denied him the right to meddle in the life of eastern churches and in their disciplinary problems. Msgr. Battifol expertly summarized this position when he wrote: "I believe that the East poorly understood Roman primacy. The East did not see in it that which Rome saw, and that which the West saw in Rome, namely, a continuity of the primacy of St. Peter. The bishop of Rome was more than the successor of St. Peter over his cathedral; he was Peter perpetuated, invested with his power and his responsibility. The East has never understood this continuity. St. Basil ignored it, as did St. Gregory of Nazianzus and St. John Chrysostom. The authority of the bishop of Rome is one of first importance, but it was never looked upon by the East as one of divine right. What a pity that such a fundamental point never was established by means of a full scale discussion and by an ecumenical council, during the centuries when unity still existed."[1]

Despite this difference of viewpoint, a *modus vivendi* had been established. The East maintained her communion with Rome and accepted several documents wherein Rome expressed her position, as, for example, at the Council of Sardica in 363, and in Pope Hormisdas' formula in 515.

1. "Cathedra Petri," *Unam Sanctam*, Vol. 4 (1938), pp. 75–76.

Rome did not intervene in the East in the same way as she did in the West; thus a certain duality in the exercise of authority was realized. On the one hand, there was direct and more frequent intervention, and on the other, there was an arbitrary role implying, nevertheless, a real power of jurisdiction. Msgr. Battifol has put forth the very enlightening idea of three zones of papal power: a suburban zone immediately responsible to Rome, a western zone outside of Italy, a zone of universal coverage but concretely representing the East, where Rome intervenes with authority but only as arbiter of the universal communion, and judges major cases.

The role played by the pope in the West, was played in the East by the titular patriarchs of the capital and the great Apostolic sees of Alexandria, Antioch, and Jerusalem. In the pentarchic system sanctioned by Justinian, the pope was considered to be the patriarch of the West and ranked first over the four eastern patriarchs. In the exercise of his supreme authority, the pope was assisted by his colleagues in the patriarchate. This system approved, on the one hand, the autonomy of the East with regard to Rome, and furthered on the other hand the development in the East of regional cultures, or several rites in the framework of various patriarchates.

In the West, on the contrary, Rome was the only Apostolic see and, in a world occupied by barbarians, it appeared to be the center and unique source of civilization. The soil was fertile; with these young and uncultured peoples, it could create a centralized and Latinized ecclesiastical life.[2]

2. The East, being more flexible, adjusted itself to an ecclesiastical organization which had more mystical bonds of unity. The West, being more legalistic, realized a stricter unity on a juridical plane.

In the East the local church was given a special prominence, whereas in Rome it was the universal interest of the Church which prevailed, with the see of Rome being considered the radiating focal point. But, in the East, Rome was given a secondary place, since universality was assured through the intermediary of the emperor, by the interpatriarchal relations and by the councils. Needless to say, once the empire were dislocated, the universal communion of the Church would be jeopardized. This is why, in the West, the sense of unity and of universality absorbed the local differences, and the power of the metropolitans and of regional councils passed on to Rome. The customs and rites of the diocese of Rome prevailed throughout Western Christendom. Several popes were tempted to use the same procedures in the East, and this zeal heightened tension and endangered unity. These seeds of disruption were to go on multiplying themselves, starting with the seventh century, while the forces of unification were wasting away.

SCHISM BEGINS TO LOOM

The equilibrium established by the pentarchy was to be shattered by a parting of the ways caused by these two factors: the weakening of the eastern patriarchates of Alexandria, Antioch, and Jerusalem; and the political separation between the papacy and the East.

The first council of Constantinople had already awarded first place of honor in the East to the see of the new capital, Constantinople. But, little by little, the bishop of the capital extended his jurisdiction over all of Asia Minor and Thracia, and even intervened in the patriarchates of Antioch and Alexandria through his permanent synod, or grouping the transient bishops in the capital, which had become the supreme religious authority in the empire.

Antioch's prestige was ruined at the Council of Ephesus in 431—since the Antiochians showed up as condemned. Alexandria's prestige was reduced at Chalcedon in 451 —where the formulas of St. Cyril of Alexandria were sacrificed. Meanwhile, Constantinople profited by canon 28 of Chalcedon, which attempted to give its bishop the same privileges as those of the bishop of Rome. The protestations of St. Leo did not stop the rise of Constantinople. The opposition at Chalcedon and the Monophysite schism which followed in the patriarchates of Alexandria and Antioch weakened the Church considerably, and both of these sees henceforth lost their predominant roles in the Church. Constantinople had become the true leader in the East and pretended to be the seat of universal Christianity; in fact, the patriarch of Constantinople, at the end of the sixth century, took the title of ecumenical patriarch despite the reproaches of St. Gregory.

The occupation of Syria and Egypt by the Arabs would further weaken that portion of the eastern Melkite patriarchates which remained Orthodox, and the obstacles placed before these patriarchates, affecting their relations with the Christian world, would reduce very noticeably their action in the general forward movement of the Church. Constantinople became the head of Eastern Orthodox Christianity, whereas the other patriarchates found themselves relegated to the rank of satellites.

The empire, however, had been reduced in size; the Semitic Orient was lost to the Arabs in the seventh century. Italy, recaptured by Justinian, was no longer attractive to the empire, now incapable of protecting it against the Lombards; it fell into the hands of Byzantium in the middle of the eighth century. The Roman Empire of the East established its quarters in Greek territory, where it became progressively Hellenized. Latin became a strange language in the new Rome.

Greek nationalism replaced Roman universalism, and the Church was to suffer from this mutilation. Whereas, at the outset of the seventh century the five patriarchal sees, including Rome, were all part of the Byzantine Empire, in the middle of the eighth century the empire was reduced to a single patriarchate, Constantinople. Isauria, the only province depending on Antioch, which escaped the capture of the Arabs, had been annexed by Constantinople. Illyricum, corresponding to the southern part of the Balkans, or western Yugoslavia, of Greek language, and depending ecclesiastically on Rome, was until then an important link between the two worlds. But in 732 an imperial decree by Leo III had joined it, as well as Sicily and Calabria, to Constantinople. The emperor even attempted to rejoin Ravenna to the patriarchate of the East, but Italy rose up to defend the pope who was persecuted by the emperor. By the middle of the eighth century the domain of the pope was entirely outside of the empire. The patriarchate of Constantinople, having become the church of the empire, which was universal by right but national in fact, attempted to impose its own tradition. The Trullan Synod, held at Constantinople in 692, arrogated to itself the right to condemn many Roman customs which were contrary to Byzantine law.

Simultaneously, there was an analogous evolution in the Western world, brought about, not by a shrinking of the Roman Empire as in the East but by the arrival of fresh elements which cooperated in creating a new world.

Rome took the initiative in the re-Christianization of western Europe by converting the Germans. She educated these people, who had been deprived of any tradition common with the East. Rome, however, still subject politically to the Byzantine Empire until the middle of the eighth century, acted as a link between the two worlds. The last pope of eastern origin died in 752. In 753 Stephen II asked for the protection of Pepin the Short against the Lombards who had invaded the Byzantine exarchate of Ravenna in 751, and were menacing Rome. Pepin refused to return the territories taken from the Lombards to Byzantium, and gave them to the pope. One could tell that the Byzantine guardianship in Rome had ceded its place to that of the Franks. Charlemagne took his role seriously, since on Christmas Eve in the year 800 he had himself crowned Emperor of the Romans by the pope.

According to the thinking of that period the emperor was the universal sovereign. Therefore the consecration of Charlemagne by the pope signified at once the decline of Byzantium and the recognition of the division of Christendom into two rival blocks. Within the medieval context of union of church and state the maintenance of ecclesiastical unity became precarious. The two Christian worlds were destined to evolve henceforth without points of contact; Greek was ignored in Rome, as Latin was in Constantinople. In 787 the last Council was held in which bishops from the East and the West rubbed elbows.

The pope, whose first role is to insure unity, found himself buried in the Western world and its politics; he was supported by the western emperor, to whom he owed fidelity. In fact, he carried on as western patriarch and his interventions in the East, less and less frequent, hardly

carried any weight, since too frequently he treated the
patriarchs as if they were his archbishops. Moreover, he
made the mistake of relying on the *False Decretals* which
were unknown to the East.[3]

The mutual isolation of the two blocks was completed
by the eleventh century. Except for ecclesiastical centralization, however, the internal life of the two churches did
not differ very much. The misunderstanding of 1054 could
have been settled, as were previous ones, if the West had
not been in the midst of a development which set it at
variance with the East. I quote Congar: "Dom Wilmart, a
profound student of ancient texts, has written that a Christian of the Fourth or Fifth Century would have felt less
bewildered by the forms of piety current in the Eleventh
Century than would his counterpart of the Eleventh Century in the forms of the Twelfth. The great break occurred
in the transition period from the one to the other century.
This change took place only in the West where, sometime
between the end of the Eleventh and the end of the
Twelfth Century, everything was somehow transformed.
This profound alteration of view did not take place in the
East where, in some respects, Christian matters are still
today what they were then—and what they were in the
West before the end of the Eleventh Century. This is a
statement that becomes clearer the better one knows the
facts. It is indeed very serious, for it concerns precisely the
moment when the schism asserted itself in a way that has
been without true remedy up to now."[4]

In this mutual parting of ways of the two worlds, there

3. The *False Decretals* are an apocryphal, canonical collection
which appeared in France about 850; in them the power of local
churches was restrained in favor of the Roman See.

4. Yves Congar, *After Nine Hundred Years* (New York: Fordham
University Press, 1959), pp. 38–39.

were many circumstantial factors. True, the East refused to recognize the new fact of the West, but the papacy, instead of linking its fate to that of the West, should have searched for a way to reunite the Byzantine Empire and the barbarian world in a new context. Unfortunately, each wanted to stay at home and live its life apart. A mutual ignorance ensued which was tantamount to an exaggerated devotion to the values of the traditions and culture of each party; this negative attitude in turn ruined the former unity respecting diversity and provoked quarrels that would lead to eventual schism.

QUARRELS AND SCHISM

The schism of 1054 was preceded by many an impasse caused by the different attitudes of easterners and westerners regarding trinitarian and christological controversies, and by the interference of emperors. Two quarrels, in particular, resulted especially from the antagonism which existed between the two blocks.

Charlemagne and the Greeks. When Charlemagne was at war with the Byzantine Empire, he strongly influenced his theologians against the traditional faith of the East. The first episode concerns the condemnation of Iconoclasm rendered by the Second Council of Nicea in 787. Charlemagne was not on speaking terms with the Greeks, at the time, because the engagement of his daughter, Rotrude, to young Constantine VI, son of Irene, who was patroness of the council, had just been broken. The Acts of the Council were transmitted in a defective translation to Charlemagne, and they gave rise to bitter criticism among the Franks. The Council of Frankfurt, which met in 794 at the request of Charlemagne, asked the pope not to approve the text of the Council of Nicea. Pope Hadrian reassured the Franks of the real orthodoxy of the Council, the Seventh Ecumenical Council. The second episode concerns the question of the *Filioque*. The oldest texts of the Nicean-Constantinople Creed, both Greek and Latin, state of the Holy Spirit *that he proceeds from the Father*. The mention of *Filioque* (*and from the Son*) was added in certain churches of the West toward the end of the sixth century.

This addition seems to have started in Spain, then to have passed into the Frankish Empire, where it was quickly accepted as the orthodox version. When dissecting the Acts of the Second Council of Nicea (787), the Frankish theologians discovered the traditional patristic version, *Who proceeds from the Father through the Son*. Pope Hadrian must have justified to them the eastern version. In 796 a petition was sent to Charlemagne, asking him to intervene in favor of inserting the *Filioque* into the Creed, but peace feelers with Byzantium were then in motion, so he tabled the matter. A few years later the dispute began again in Jerusalem among the Sabaite monks and the Frankish monks of Mount Olive who, having returned from a mission to the court of Charlemagne, started to sing the Creed with the *Filioque*. Patriarch Thomas of Jerusalem referred the matter to Pope St. Leo III. Charlemagne became involved—hostilities had started up again with the Greeks in 806. The Council of Aix-la-Chapelle, held in 809 at the instigation of the emperor, decided to send a mission to Rome to ask the pope to impose the insertion of the *Filioque* into the Creed. St. Leo refused, and ordered the placing of two silver plaques at the entrance of the Confession of St. Peter, showing the Creed, both in Greek and Latin, without the *Filioque*. This was a stroke of wisdom. At Rome the Creed was still sung as in Constantinople, until 1014, at which date Pope Benedict VIII inserted the *Filioque* in the Roman liturgy text to please Emperor Henry II.

The matter of the *Filioque* was to be taken up again, this time against the Latins by the patriarch Photius in his quarrel with Pope Nicholas I.

The Photian Schism. Despite the political break with Byzantium the papacy had maintained considerable prestige in the East until the middle of the ninth century, because it had supported monks who were partial to the image cult in their battle against the iconoclast emperors. But the Photian quarrel and the difficult years for the papacy, which started immediately after it, were to undermine the authority of the papacy significantly.

Photius, who embodied the finer and more subtle things of Byzantium, found himself confronted in Rome with Nicholas I (858–867), the most energetic, the roughest, and the most rigid upholder of the question of papal rights and Roman prestige.[5] Photius, a layman, had been elevated much against his will to the patriarchal see in 858 by order of the emperor to replace Patriarch Ignatius, who had been judged undesirable by the government. This was not a very canonical procedure, but it had been referred to Byzantium. Any one else but Ignatius would have retired, but he was obstinate and refused to abdicate, although some pretext to support his deposition was found at a synod in 859. In order to establish his credentials, Photius sent his synodal letters to the eastern patriarchs and to the pope. Nicholas I, who had not received any word from Ignatius, sent a delegation to Constantinople for

5. Roman primacy had taken on a new aspect in Rome, derived for the most part from the false canonical collection then in vogue, namely the *False Decretals* and the *False Isidoreans*.

information. The legates were persuaded to favor Photius. They approved the condemnation of Ignatius at the Council of 861. Nicholas I, however, contravened these legates, refused to recognize Photius, and treated him as a scoundrel and an imposter. At this moment Ignatius and his followers, all men of high integrity, appealed to Rome. The Roman Synod of 863 reduced Photius and all those ordained by him to laymen. These decisions reflected a misunderstanding of the state of things existing in Byzantium. The Byzantine patriarch was not to be treated like the metropolitans of the Carolingian Empire. Photius remained head of Constantinople.

This matter was being settled, when the Bulgarian affair halted the process. At that time, Bulgaria was embracing Christianity, thanks to the influence of Byzantine missionaries; King Boris, whose godfather was Emperor Michael III, was baptized in Constantinople in 864.

Photius sent several priests into Bulgaria to complete the evangelization of the people, but he did not give Boris the autonomous hierarchy he wanted. The dissatisfied king delegated an ambassador to Rome in 866, with the hope of obtaining from Nicholas I that which Photius had refused to give him. The pope, completely enraptured with the thought of regaining a footing in a land formerly dependent directly on Rome, sent a delegation to Bulgaria which imposed the rejection of Byzantine practices, expelled the Greek missionaries, and reconfirmed those who had been baptized and confirmed by eastern priests.

Photius had remained silent after 863, but he could not tolerate this effrontery directed against his church. Irritated and bitter, he wrote a virulent encyclical, in 867, addressed to the faithful of his oriental patriarchate. In it he called them to Constantinople to judge Pope Nicholas I. In this

letter he condemned the Latin doctrine of the *Filioque*.
He wrote to the Western Emperor, Louis II, at the same
time, to ask him to remove Nicholas I from the pontifical
throne. The Council of 867 deposed and excommunicated
the pope. Envoys were sent to notify Louis II and the
pope of the sentence, but the latter died before the Byzantine delegation arrived, and Photius lost his see in a
coup d'état, which defeated his protector, Emperor Michael III.

The next emperor, Basil I, reinstated Ignatius to the
patriarchal see, and wanted to restore the entente with
Rome. The Council of 869, the Fourth of Constantinople,
condemned Photius. At the tenth session in a theatrical
coup the Bulgarian delegation came to offer its country's
pledges of reunion with the see of Constantinople. Despite
the protests of the pontifical envoys, the delegates from the
Melkite patriarchs, called by Ignatius to serve as arbiters
in the conflict, recognized the rights of Constantinople
over Bulgaria. Ignatius immediately consecrated an archbishop for Bulgaria. Later on he consecrated ten more. The
Latin missionaries were expelled from Bulgaria. Despite
threats of excommunication Ignatius held firm to his position. Just as the two sees were on the brink of another
split, Ignatius died in 877, and was replaced by Photius.
At the Council of 879–880, held at Constantinople in the
presence of the pontifical legates, Photius entered into
communion with Rome and was recognized as Patriarch of
Constantinople. Everything indicates that Photius died
while officially in this communion. These conciliatory
measures had been the work of Pope John VIII, who
needed the help of Emperor Basil against the incursions of
the Saracens in Italy because the Carolingian Empire was
in full decline.

The result of this whole affair, as far as Rome is concerned, is not very clear. During the tenth century the papacy went through a difficult period, while Byzantium reached its peak, and outstanding patriarchs held the see of Constantinople. The latter treated the popes as colleagues, and not as hierarchical superiors. Some misunderstandings arose, but Constantinople easily adjusted itself to a canonical break with Rome, which merely amounted to omitting the pope's name from the liturgy. One of the quarrels, although not greater than the others, was not followed by a reconciliation, the quarrel of 1054.

The Schism of 1054 Under Cerularius. When Michael Cerularius became head of the see of Constantinople (1043), the canonical relations between the two Romes had been interrupted for approximately twenty years; hence, he was not required to send his synodal letter to the pope. He was not bothered by this state of affairs and did not care to change it.

A political alliance, however, was being formed between Byzantium, the pope, and the Germanic emperor, in order to defend Italy against the Normans—the Byzantines had regained a footing in southern Italy with Basil I, at the end of the ninth century. In order to shake things up, Cerularius closed the Latin churches of Constantinople and requested Leo, Archbishop of Bulgaria, to address a manifesto to John, Latin Bishop of Trani in Apulia, against the Latin usages considered to be illegitimate and contrary to Apostolic tradition. The Latin church was urgently requested to give up these practices.

The letter came to Pope Leo IX, who requested Cardinal Humbert to prepare a lengthy accusation containing incriminations against the church of Constantinople. The document, addressed to Michael, Bishop of Constantinople, and to Leo, Bishop of Achrida, happily was never delivered, because in the meantime, the Byzantine army and the pontifical army were separately defeated by the Normans; hence, there was now a pressing need to strength the military alliance. Consequently the Byzantine Duke of Italy, Argyros, sent Bishop John of Trani to Constantinople with orders to end the sterile disputes and to rebuild political and religious unity. The emperor and the patriarch wrote conciliatory letters to the pope. The latter sent a delegation, headed by Cardinal Humbert, with new letters in which Patriarch Cerularius was accused and summoned to make the following solemn and public retraction: "Such is the position of Rome: Were a church to exist in this world, that would manifest its discord with the Church of Rome, it would no longer be a church, but a mere gathering of heretics, a collection of schismatics, and a synagogue of Satan."

This harsh tone was not conducive to appeasing the proud patriarch. Cerularius convinced himself that the letter was not from the pope but rather from his enemy, Argyros. Also, upon learning of the death of Leo IX, he thought that the power of the legates was nullified—if, in reality, any power had been conferred upon them at all. For himself, his conduct toward them would be simple; he would ignore them. Meanwhile, Humbert and the monks of the capital lost themselves in sterile polemics. Then, confronted with the obstinacy of the patriarch who refused to see them, the legates decided to leave while preparing the excommunication of Cerularius. On Saturday, July 16, 1054, before the celebration of the sacred liturgy at St. Sophia they placed the letter of excommunication on the main altar, in full view of the clergy and the people. The following Sunday, July 24, the

Permanent Synod of Constantinople hurled an anathema
at this impious libel "in which men, coming from the West
into the city protected by God, attempted to pervert its
Orthodoxy." The legates alone were incriminated, but the
dissolution of these negotiations would sustain the separation of these two sees even to our day.

THE DEEPENING OF THE SCHISM AND
EFFORTS FOR REUNION

The schism of 1054 did not have the rigidity nor the
depth which it has today. Life in Byzantium went on
as it had before, and the writers of that period hardly
mentioned the event. The extreme intolerance for the
Latin rite, amply demonstrated by Cerularius, was not
adopted by the other eastern bishops. For a long time the
eastern patriarchates with the Slavonic churches remained
in communion with Rome without severing ties with
Constantinople. The rapport between Rome and the Greek
monasteries of Sinai and Patmos was maintained for centuries; likewise, the Latin monasteries, established in Constantinople or at Athos, maintained ties with the local
hierarchies. The causes of induration can be attributed to
the Crusades and to the marked Scholasticism of theology
and of dogma in the West.

The Fourth Crusade. As a result of the Fourth Crusade
the Orient was subjected to a foreign occupation which
was a profound blow to the national pride and religious
faith of the Greeks. The see of Constantinople was marked
with violent bloodshed in 1204 at the hands of the Frankish knights. Innocent III energetically blamed, in cutting
terms, these "Latins whom the Greeks have every right to
detest, because they have bathed themselves in the blood

of Christians, sparing neither religion, nor age, nor sex
. . . They have lifted their hands against the treasures of
the churches, defiled the sanctuaries, etc."

A Latin emperor was installed at Constantinople, and
the country was divided into dukedoms and counties according to the feudal system. The church was also organized to benefit the Latins; a Latin patriarch was enthroned
at Constantinople, since the Greek patriarch had abdicated.
At his death the Greeks did not obtain permission to name
his successor. In the provinces the Greek hierarchy and
the clergy were maintained only if they favored reunion.
The Greek bishops were subject to Latin bishops and were
treated as their curates. They pledged obedience not only
to the pope, but also to the Latin archbishop. They were
required to take this oath in accordance with the prestation
ritual of a feudal vassal. A great deal of pressure was ex-
erted on the East to force her to acquiesce to western theology, and to submit herself to its jurisdiction; for this end,
some legates started a veritable rule of terror.

As a result of the Fourth Crusade, which humiliated a
nation and the Church, and caused the violation of con-
sciences, the Latins aroused strong feelings of bitterness.
This bitterness was strengthened by the phenomenon of a
general evolution in the life of the Church in the West during the twelfth and thirteenth centuries, liturgically, as
well as canonically and theologically, as mentioned earlier.
The schism no longer translated itself, as in the ninth or
even the eleventh century, into a simple omission of the
pope's name in the diptychs. From that time on the people
felt a live animosity towards Latins, and regarded the "innovations" of these Latins as "heresies."

For political reasons all attempts to restore religious
unity with the West, in general, fell to the emperors.

As late as 1330 these efforts were motivated by a fear of a new Latin crusade against Constantinople. As a result, the emperors attempted to get help from the West against the Turks. The hierarchy yielded to this maneuver, partially because of a certain complaisance, and partially because of a real sincerity. But it was the people who held unity in check. Among the various movements toward unity, two were crowned with short-lived success: the Council of Lyons in 1274, and the Council of Florence in 1439.

The Unity of Lyons. The unity established at Lyons in 1274 lasted only eight years. It was mostly the work of Emperor Michael Palaeologus VIII, who recaptured Constantinople from the Latins, and put an end to their empire in 1261. But on both sides this unity was not fully desired; in Byzantium, it brought together many powerful opponents who were often objects of violence and cruelty. In Rome the successors of Gregory I gave evidence of a supreme incomprehension. The decisions of the Council of Lyons already met with obstacles to their acceptance, although Patriarch Vekkos made every sincere effort to show that unity was not only good for the advantages it produced, but was valid in its very principle. The new popes wanted to introduce some disagreeable conditions, not foreseen by the council, such as a special oath to be imposed on all the clergy, and the introduction of the *Filioque* into the Creed. Nicholas III was astonished when the Byzantine bishops did not request to be released from their excommunication as schismatics, and when they did not request confirmation of their duties. During this time Charles of Anjou, ruler of the Two Sicilies, prepared a crusade against Byzantium. Martin IV (1282–1285), friend

of Charles, favored these projects, and slighted the envoys of Michael VIII who brought him the congratu-
lations of their master on the occasion of Michael's crown-
ing. The irritated emperor was on the verge of dissolving
the union, but he was content merely to exclude the
pope's name from the diptychs. Martin IV replied with an
excommunication in 1281, which was renewed in 1282
after the Sicilian Vespers at which Michael III had been
present. The emperor died late in 1282, and his son,
Andronicus II (1282–1328) deposed the Patriarch, Vekkos, and destroyed the unity.

During the fourteenth century various measures were
undertaken to heal the schism. The Byzantines, pressured
by the Turkish advance in Asia Minor and the Balkans,
asked for the cooperation of the Christian West against
the infidels; the papacy imposed religious unity as a preliminary condition to the granting of this requested assistance. After various steps, which brought about negative
results, it was nevertheless possible to convoke the Council
of Florence in 1439.

Unity of Florence. The initiative of the Council returned to Emperor John VII (1425–1448), who wanted
to try his last chance to save the hard-pressed empire. Pope
Eugene IV also saw, in view of the schismatic Council
of Basel, that a meeting of the council with the Greeks
would mean enhancing his prestige. The meeting began
at Ferrara in 1438, but the plague and financial difficulties
forced the Council to move to Florence. They had waited
in vain for the arrival of western princes for six months,
and mixed commissions were created to discuss the controversial points which existed between the two churches.
On the Greek side the most eminent theologians favorable

to unity were: Bessarion, Metropolitan of Nicea, and Isidore, Metropolitan of Kiev; the most obstinate adversary was Mark of Ephesus. After several months of discussion devoted almost exclusively to the question of the *Filioque,* some formulations of agreement were reached, and the doctrines of the two churches remained basically alike. Roman primacy was recognized, and the rights and privileges of the patriarchs of the East were safeguarded. The Decree of Unity was signed on July 6, 1439. Mark of Ephesus and a few other Greeks abstained.

Upon their return the fathers of the Council were poorly received at Constantinople, and the bishops denied their signatures. Unity was officially maintained until the death of John VIII, but his son, Constantine XI, hesitated to proclaim it. In 1450 a synod would have condemned the unity of Florence and deposed the Patriarch, Gregory Mammas, who fled to Rome. In 1451, however, Mohammed II began his reign and became a menace to the capital. Constantine contacted the pope to solicit help against the Turks, and promised to accept the Council of Florence. The pope sent him two hundred men with Cardinal Isidore of Kiev. On December 12, 1452, unity was proclaimed anew at St. Sophia, where the liturgy was celebrated by the Greeks and the Latins, with a remembrance of the pope and the Patriarch, Gregory. On May 29, 1453, Constantinople fell into the hands of the Turks, and unity was out of the question.

The unities of Lyons and Florence did not succeed, because they were negotiated by diplomats without any preparation made by the Church. Neither the Greeks nor the Latins made an effort to come out of their mutual estrangement, and Christian people had remained perfect strangers to the dialogue started at these two councils.

AFTER FLORENCE

Rome and Orthodoxy. After the conquest of Constantinople by the Ottomans general attempts at unity were no longer possible, and in 1484 a general Orthodox synod, held in the capital, officially condemned the unity of Florence. Despite the continuation of the schism, however, relations between the two churches did not reflect the coolness and rigidity found in the nineteenth and twentieth centuries. Between eastern and western churches some ties remained that were close and friendly; several patriarchs insisted on sending their nephews to the Greek College founded in Rome by Gregory XIII, and many assured the pope of their adherence to Roman primacy. The Latin missionaries, such as the Capuchins, the Jesuits, and the Carmelites established at Constantinople ever since the sixteenth century, and in the Levant since the beginning of the seventeenth century, were well received by their local hierarchies. They preached freely in the Orthodox churches and requested permission from Greek bishops to hear confessions.

The following tells how a Jesuit missionary during the middle of the seventeenth century explained his method of hearing the confessions of the Orthodox: "When a Greek comes to us for confession, we ask him if he believes all that the Greek Fathers, Basil, Athanasius, Gregory, Chrysostom, Damascene, and others taught. He answers, 'Yes.' Their Creed moreover, being the same as ours except for the word *Filioque,* which we maintain to be a simple declaration of the Creed and not an addition, we ask him if he understands the Creed in the same sense as that of the holy councils and Fathers of the Church; he answers, 'Yes.' Whereupon, we hear his confession and

give him absolution . . . When learned men come to confession to us, we question them more extensively on all
controversial points, and have them renounce their errors
insofar as it is necessary."[6]

It was not necessary to leave the ecclesiastical community, for this was the proper method of eliminating all
prejudice against the Latins, and of preparing minds for
a general unity. Unfortunately, relations between the two
churches were soon to deteriorate and to worsen. The most
deep-rooted cause of this alienation was the establishment
of pro-unity elements in particular communities.

In territories existing under a Catholic regime, the Jesuit
apostolate helped to create a unity analogous to that of
Florence. This was maintained by the ensemble of the
hierarchy gathered in synod. Such was the unity of Brest in
1595, when the Ukrainians lived in a Lithuano-Polish state,
and such was the unity of the Synod of Alba-Julia in
1617, when Rumanians of Transylvania lived in the
Austro-Hungarian Empire. The unity of these territories,
which remained strangers to the Ottoman Empire and to
the influence of the ecumenical patriarchate, did not provoke the same feeling in the Greeks as the success of
Catholicism had done in the patriarch of Antioch. This
success, owing to the work of the missionaries and the
French protectorate, brought about a lively reaction from
the Greeks of Constantinople and affected a halt in the
move towards unity. The sultan's order prohibited the
missionaries from exercising their ministry among the
Orientals. Against the Syrian Patriarch, elected by Catholics in 1724 (Cyril Tanas VI), Constantinople set up a
Greek, who persecuted the Catholics by favoring the Turks.

6. Extract from a statement entitled "The Jesuits in Levant about
1650" which appeared in *L'unité de l'Eglise*, No. 64, p. 934.

The Catholic patriarch escaped to Lebanon where an internal autonomy sheltered him from the pressure of Constantinople.

In 1729 a decree from the Sacred Congregation of Propaganda prohibited Catholics from participating in Orthodox religious services. This was tantamount to instituting a separation of the two communities and to blessing a duplication of hierarchy. The establishment of the United Oriental Churches contributed to the hardening of the schism. It removed from the Orthodox community all the elements favoring a rapprochement with Rome. As a result, Catholicism gained little, and the leaven was separated from the dough. It deeply wounded the Orthodox, and created in them a live mistrust in the papacy, of the Latin missionary efforts in the East, and of all moves toward unity. Rome, in setting up this Catholic hierarchy, appeared to look upon it as heir to the ancient Oriental church. Relations of Rome with the separated brethren could hardly escape this blow. The policy of forced conversion to Orthodoxy, pursued by Czar Nicholas I towards Ukrainian Uniates, also led Rome to forbid more definitively the intercommunion between Catholics and Orthodox.

The Greeks bolstered their strength, and in their profound mistrust, remained deaf to all the advances of Pius IX and Leo XIII, which were looked upon as maneuvers to use the humiliated Oriental church. They refused to respond to an invitation to attend Vatican I (1869), and the Patriarch of Constantinople, Anthimos VII, replied violently to the unionist encyclical of Leo XIII *Praeclara Gratulationis* (1894). The chilling of relations between the two churches, in the nineteenth century, was complete in the triumph of Ultramontanism against Gallican and Febronian ideas, the definitions of the Vatican Council and because of the closed Europeanism which characterized the nineteenth century. One way or another, the ground suitable for the fruition of the dialogue was not sufficiently prepared.

Rome and the United Oriental Churches. The united Oriental communities themselves were never acknowledged by the group of western Catholics who continued to ignore them, to suspect them, and to bully them. Some went so far as to fight them openly on their own grounds. After taking part in the uniting of the oriental Churches, the Latin missionaries, working in the East, no longer cooperated in their development but labored to attract older Catholics and those who had been converted from Orthodoxy to the Latin rite. To this end they organized themselves hierarchically and ignored the Oriental churches. A person of very high ecclesiastical rank said privately, a few years ago, to a custodian of the Holy Land: "Let them Latinize. As long as they are not Latins, the root of the schism will live on." The popes however, opposed such procedures; Urban VIII, in 1624, forbade Ukrainians to change to the Latin rite; Benedict XIV, in 1743, rose up against the passing of the Greek Melkites to the Latin rite which had been favored by the Franciscans of Damascus. "We further forbid, again, each and every Greek Catholic to change to the Latin rite. We forbid, as well, all missionaries, under penalty of sanctions mentioned further, and others which we withhold *arbitrio nostro,* to dare to persuade anyone to change over to the Latin rite or even to allow those who desire to do so without prior advice from the Holy See." But this law was poorly observed, and the Sacred Congregation of Propaganda often intervened. The foundation of a Latin patriarchate at Jerusalem in 1847 was the beginning of a systematic Latinization. Leo XIII reacted strongly, and on November 30, 1894, he published the encyclical *Orientalium dignitas,* which aimed to restore the value of the dignity of Oriental churches and the necessity of preserving oriental rites in their entirety. "In order to bring about the best way to reconciliation, the most important thing it seems to us, is to direct our attention and our care to the preservation of the particular discipline of the East, which, of course, we have always done. Also, we have prescribed for the colleges recently established in those countries and for those to come the greatest respect and exact observation of the rites which the students must know and practice. Their maintenance, in fact, is more important than we realize. The august antiquity which ennobles the various rites is the ornament of the whole Church and attests to the divine unity of the Catholic faith. They show forth more clearly to the principal churches of the East their apostolic origin and, at the same time, illustrate their intimate union with the Church of Rome, which flows from the principle of Christianity. Nothing, in fact, better demonstrates the catholicity of the Church of God than the singular homage of these ceremonies of different forms, celebrated in languages venerated by antiquity, and consecrated by the usage which the Apostles and the Fathers made thereof.

"In the past Western missionaries had not always taken into account these wise principles, and the oriental patriarchs had more than once advised Rome of their impetuous Latinizing attempts. In order to see the whole picture and to evaluate it, we have deemed it useful to call to Rome recently these same patriarchs and to have an understanding with them.

"We have often brought them together with some of our beloved cardinal sons of the Holy Roman Church to deliberate in our presence. After having thoroughly studied what had been prepared and discussed at these meetings, we have resolved to make more explicit, all encompassing, and consistent with the new situation of these peoples the prescriptions of the Constitution of Benedict XIV. We shall draw therefrom the following principle: Latin priests are sent into these regions by the Apostolic See solely to be helpers and supporters. Therefore, it is necessary that, as they use power given to them, they do not hold any prejudice against the jurisdiction of these ordinaries and do not reduce the number of their subjects." The pope then gave precise prescriptions for missionaries and established some severe sanctions against the Latinizers.

But it would seem that this encyclical had no more success than *Rerum Novarum*. Both of them, though in different ways, did not agree with the good conscience of the pious conservatives. Here are a few excerpts from a report sent to the Holy See in 1920 by the Melkite Patriarch, Dimitri Cadi, who was otherwise very sympathetic towards the West.

". . . The third cause of difficulty—in many ways the most important because of its immediate consequences—is the absolute indifference of the missionaries to our rites, our liturgical customs, and our disciplinary rules . . . the missionaries practically conduct themselves as though the oriental rite was nonexistent. They make no effort whatsoever to understand it. This indifference to the oriental rite, which at times becomes a true aversion, is more palpable when the order or congregation is of a narrow in-

tellectual culture . . . These persons are pious and har-
bor no evil intentions, but they feel that the oriental rite
is tolerated by the popes because there is no other choice.
They also feel that nothing is to be gained by adapting it
for their own. They think it a pious endeavor to insist on
Latin practices as much as possible because in their eyes
these alone insure true piety and perseverance in the
Catholic faith.

"The dissidents who understand perfectly the promises
made by the popes, which the Oriental clergy does not
hesitate to recall from time to time, are witnesses to
this way of acting and draw a perfect parallel between
theory and practice. The result, from the standpoint of the
Catholic apostolate, is twofold: First, the missionaries make
no conversions, or make very few . . . Second, this conduct weakens our own churches. The objective visualized
by Leo XIII was not reached . . . We see this distressing
withdrawal of the majority of our youth from our churches,
and our educated class, moved by a craze which is only too
well encouraged, tends to do the same."

Pius XI understood that all the decrees would prove use-
less, if the general mentality of the Latin West was
not changed. The parochial milieu in which the missionaries were born and the religious congregations who
trained them, completely ignored the East and encouraged
no sympathy towards it. Within the Latin Church the
primary work in the search for unity consisted of the
exigency to increase the knowledge and esteem of the
Christian Orient.

Pius XI encouraged Eastern studies and tried to interest
all bishops to do the same. In 1924 he wrote to Archbishop Précan, of Olmuz in Czechoslovakia, on the

occasion of the Congress for the Orient: "One of the principal aims of this Congress is the acquisition of new knowledge concerning the historical facts and the vicissitudes of
nations, the habits and customs of Oriental peoples, and
the respectable rites or institutions of their churches . . .
We sincerely hope that the holy resolutions of similar
congresses will greatly help to stamp out many doubts and
errors, monstrous at times, which took root among the people concerning everything related to the history of the religious life of the East."

Pius XI published a special encyclical *Rerum Oriental-*
ium on September 8, 1928, to promote oriental studies:
"To favor the study and profound knowledge of oriental
questions, not only among the faithful but especially
among the priests, had been during the past centuries the
great desire of our predecessors. This is a fact which cannot escape the attention even of a superficial reader of the
annals of the Church. In fact, our predecessors were not
ignorant of the truth that many previous evils, and the
deplorable schism which had torn so many flourishing
churches away from unity, ensued, first of all, as the
fatal consequence of ignorance and mutual contempt of
peoples, and of prejudices resulting from long animosities.
It is impossible, therefore, ever to remedy so many evils, if
we do not succeed in removing these obstacles.

"This is why, since we must not neglect anything conducive either to bringing back to the unity of the true
Church of Christ such an important portion of her flock,
or to developing charity towards those who, in the diversity
of rites, adhere intimately to the heart and soul of the
Roman Church and the vicar of Christ, we sincerely beg
each one of you, venerable brethren, to select one of your
priests, who, being well informed concerning Oriental

questions, will be ready to explain them adequately to the students of your seminaries."

In his encyclical *Ecclesiam Dei,* published on November 12, 1923, Pius XI was insisting on the necessity of serious scientific work, in order to learn to know one another better and to come to a deeper love for one another: "Latins must acquire more complete and deeper notions of oriental customs and things. St. Josaphat (Ukrainian Bishop, and martyr for unity, whose tercentenary was being commemorated) had a perfect knowledge thereof, and this is what made his apostolate so fruitful . . . We maintain, in fact, as certain, that an exact knowledge of things will bring about an equitable appreciation of persons, and, at the same time, a sincere good will."

The thrust given by Pius XI is now beginning to reap its fruits. The work of the Commission for Oriental Churches, of Istina, and of the ecumenical center at the monastery of Chevetogne joined with the prestige of the oriental churches united to Rome has made it possible for westerners to increase their knowledge of the Orient. The process has begun. The Western world is beginning to welcome things Eastern with curiosity and sympathy, and soon this movement will reach the various centers. We must be thankful to the modern popes for having done so much for the preservation of oriental rites despite strong opposing currents in the West and in the Curia.

But, unfortunately, these rites no longer have profound meaning for the Uniates, who have become Latinized. The larger portion of our elite was trained in schools created by Latin missionaries, where no oriental education was given, either from an ecclesiastical or from a national point of view. Seminaries were maintained for the most part by Latin missionaries; our priests studied with the help of

Latin theology textbooks, and the eastern rite no longer had deep roots in them, since they had been trained in Western methods of spirituality.

Maximos IV Saigh, Melkite Patriarch of Antioch, made the following remarks during a lecture given at Düsseldorf on August 9, 1960:[7] "The founders of Uniatism respected only the rites of the East. As for the rest, they often tried to remove the best from the East, in order to present to it or to impose upon it that which the West had of lesser quality. The West, as a whole, has not yet fully realized that there is in the East, besides liturgical rites, other great spiritual, artistic, theological, and institutional treasures to be safeguarded for the good of the whole Church. . . . Accordingly, it worked to destroy everything which did not resemble it; and one must admit that it succeeded fairly well, since in most of the eastern Catholic communities, except for liturgical rites nothing resembles the West more than this united East. Therefore, this model of unity does not, as we understand it, facilitate our mission."

An adequate understanding of this infringement will result from a comprehension not only of the sociological and cultural reasons for it but also from the knowledge that at the time these unions came into being the West possessed a limited notion of liturgy. "Considered," says Father Congar, "in its most limited sense, 'rite' would be nothing more than an external system, no matter what its content; a certain conviction, considered as existing in itself and universally valid which could be transferred indifferently from one linguistic group to another, from one 'rite' to another. Such a transfer would

7. *Vers l'unité chrétienne,* XIII, 52.

involve no more than a substitution of another language, different rubrics and ceremonies. On the other hand, we can understand the notion of 'rite' in a much wider and deeper sense. In that case, 'rite' encompasses the totality of forms and symbols by which a community gives complete expression to, and lives its Christian faith. It is then not merely a collection of liturgical rubrics but includes the theology as well as the whole manner of organization of the ecclesiastical and religious life of a people. Fundamentally, then, it is the Christian life itself, collectively perceived and felt in a particular way and which creates for itself its own personal, communal manner of expression. . . From this it follows that although in the West the word 'rite' is taken in the narrow sense, it is understood in a broader and deeper sense in the East."[8] Taken in this wide sense, we can say that, in general, the eastern rites have not been fully respected in the United eastern Churches.[9]

More significant is the following: the patriarchal and synodal character proper to the oriental church has not been fully respected. At the Council of Florence, after the declaration of the primacy of the Roman Pontiff, was added the phrase: "there being retained the privileges and

8. Yves Congar, *op. cit.*, pp. 34–36.
9. The fault is not directly imputable to the West itself. Formerly many eastern Catholics considered it an honor to get as close as possible to the Latins, because they were no longer nourished by their own tradition. We must note that the Melkite Catholic church best resisted the Latinizing current which influenced the other Eastern Catholic communities.

The feeling of belonging to the vast Byzantine world, and the patriarchal dignity attached to its head, to the exclusion of the other Catholic Byzantine groups, no doubt explains the situation. But there is also reason to recall that these patriarchs were often in conflict with apostolic delegates.

the rights of the patriarchs of the East." At the Vatican Council, the Melkite Patriarch, Gregory Youssef, added the same clause to his signature. After this Council, papal declarations did not lose sight of these principles.

Pope Leo XIII said, when speaking to the Orthodox: "Nor is there any reason for you to fear on that account that We or any of Our successors will ever diminish your rights, the privileges of your patriarchs, or the established ritual of any of your churches. It has been and always will be the intent and tradition of the Apostolic See, to make a large allowance, in all that is right and good, for the primitive traditions and special customs of every nation."[10] And elsewhere: "From all evidence, it would not be fitting, nor would it be at all proper, that something be lacking in the patriarchal power among Catholics, concerning that which constitutes its prestige and its dignity among non-Catholics."[11] And again: "We want nothing to be revoked or diminished in the rights, privileges, duties, and competency of the patriarch."[12]

Pius XII repeated the same affirmations. "On this occasion, we shall observe that the Orientals must not fear that, as a result of the restoration of the unity of faith and of government, they must abandon their rites or their legitimate customs. That is what our predecessors have declared and widely proclaimed, more than once, in saying to the Orientals: Nor is there any reason for you to fear on that account that We or any of Our successors will ever diminish your rights, the privileges of your patriarchs, or the established ritual of any of your churches."[13] Despite all

10. Encyclical *Praeclara Gratulationis* of June 20, 1894.
11. Encyclical *Auspicia Rerum* of March 19, 1896.
12. Encyclical *Omnibus Compertum* of July 21, 1900.
13. Encyclical *Orientalium Omnes* addressed to the Ukrainians in December 1945.

these declarations, the Roman organizing and centralizing spirit led to the transfer of the essential of patriarchal power to Roman congregations. The only truly patriarchal elements which remained were so subjected to preliminary authorizations and final approvals, that the patriarchal reality was emptied of its meaning.

We know that the eastern Catholics started out by being subjects of the Sacred Congregation of Propaganda. In 1862 Pius IX created a special commission, within this congregation, to deal with oriental affairs. Benedict XV, in 1917, released them from the Congregation of Propaganda, and established the Oriental Congregation for them. In 1938 Pius XI even placed Latins who had settled in the East under this Commission.[14] We know, of course, that the code of canon law, published in 1917, deals only with the Latin church. The codification for the Oriental church is still in process, but many sections have already appeared. Despite the great merits of this work, the Catholic orientalists who were concerned about their Orthodox brethren were disappointed. Cardinal Massimi, President of the Commission for Codification, had reassured them, by declaring to the Melkite Patriarch Cyril IX and his followers during a visit to Rome in 1939: "When this code appears, every Orthodox who will see it, will shout: yes, truly, this is our code, this is our law, it is the voice of our fathers."

But this Code appeared to them, in many respects, to be

14. The Congregation for the Oriental Church has, under the presidency of the Sovereign Pontiff himself, full and exclusive jurisdiction in the following countries: Egypt, the peninsula of Sinai, Erythrea, the northern part of Ethiopia, Southern Albania, Bulgaria, Cyprus, Greece, the Dodecanese, Iran, Iraq, Lebanon, Palestine, Syria, Transjordan, and the Turkish Republic. (Motu proprio *Sancta Dei Ecclesia* of March 26, 1938.)

Latinized. Here is what Patriarch Maximos IV Saigh said, in his lecture at Düsseldorf: "To cite the example of the recent codification of Oriental canon law prepared in Rome, we would do well to consider with regret that, despite an impressive critical, formal preparation, a terminology inspired by Oriental sources, and a commendable effort, the basis of this codification unfortunately does, nonetheless, Latinize. This fault is not entirely due to the technicians who worked on it. It can be attributed as well to the spirit which permeates the milieu in which this work was done. For this milieu the ideal remains achieving the closest possible union both in essence and form, with the law of the Latin Church. The institutions proper to the East, such as the patriarchal institutions, for example, are tolerated as exceptions, and are limited as strictly as possible, if not completely and skillfully emptied of their meaning. They are practically neutralized as a result of exaggerated administrative centralization."[15]

Basically, Rome wants to spread its administration in the East, to the same degree that it administers the West, by applying the oriental code on one, and the Latin code on the other. But, is this not a decoy? What is the oriental law, if not the non-Roman law which came out of the Eastern conciliar meetings and patriarchal decrees? Can a legislation, elaborated by Rome, minimizing the real patriarchal power and trying to meet the demands of the oriental hierarchy, still be called "oriental"?

The Catholic Melkite hierarchy, conscious of its responsibility and of the danger which this legislation places in the path of the true catholicity of the Church, and of the cause of unity in the East, met in synod at Cairo, in

February 1958, and addressed a request to His Holiness Pope Pius XII. This request was later completed by observations submitted to His Holiness Pope John XXIII in May, 1959. The reign of His Holiness Pope John XXIII opened a new era of appeasement. Great hopes were placed on the ecumenical council to enable the Church to approach the problem of unity of all Christians.

The institution of the Secretariat for Promoting Christian Unity, with its own section for the East, the recent trip of His Holiness Pope Paul VI to Jerusalem, and his meeting near Calvary with His Holiness Athenagoras, Ecumenical Patriarch, the decision of the Pan-Orthodox Assembly of Rhodes to hasten the start of the dialogue with Rome, all reflect the new spirit of charity and unity, which characterizes the relationships between the two churches. But the efforts of the heads of the hierarchy would amount to naught, if all Christians were not to collaborate by welcoming others and by praying.

CHAPTER VIII · MEANING AND VALUE OF THE CHRISTIAN ORIENT

WHAT IS THE ORIENT?

THE CHURCH OF CHRIST, one, holy, catholic, apostolic, without ceasing to be the same, has presented different and varied faces through the ages. The Church of the twentieth century presents itself differently from that of the thirteenth or of the fourth century in her organization, her discipline, her theology, and in her liturgy, even though it remains the same Church of Christ. This is easily understandable, since the Church is constantly incorporated into human society, and ecclesiological life adorns itself with culture. A man of the twentieth century differs from one of the thirteenth or of the fourth century, yet, basically man is always the same and his salvation is unique.

However, if there is a modern man and an ancient man, there is also an eastern man and a western man; the Church, in becoming alive in these men, took on different appearances. There is an eastern Catholicism as there is a western Catholicism. Both are equally valid and authentic. They are what they are independently of the separation;

it is not the schism which has made the East different from the West.

There are already some varieties within Western Catholicism; we speak of German Catholicism, of French and Spanish Catholicism, etc. These important realities contain ethnic, social, cultural, historical and religious differences which are difficult to specify. We also find the various schools of spirituality such as the Benedictine School, the Carmelite School, the French School, the Ignatian School, all of which are Apostolic and can lead to holiness. We find analogous differences in theology, religious art and, on a lower scale, in liturgy, as, for example, in the Ambrosian, Mozarabic, and the Lyonnaise rites.

The difference between East and West is more radical still. The difference is on the ecclesiological plane. According to the Catholic Melkite writer, O. Kéramé, "The Oriental Church is a Church born directly of the Apostles. It has grown, developed, conquered entire nations for Christ, established its law, and regulated the order of its public prayer, its sacraments, its sacrifice of the Mass without Roman intervention. In short, it is the Church in its non-Roman aspect. This does not mean that it is anti-Roman, or devoid of all Roman influence. Quite the contrary. This Oriental Church has lived a life in common with the Latin Church and both have experienced a profound unity. Thus the Oriental Church is authentically Catholic because she achieved an organization and development which may best be described as non-Roman in its historical externals."[1]

Oriental Catholicism is a patriarchal Catholicism, born on the spot, nourished by local Apostolic tradition and or-

1. O. Kéramé, "Le prochain concile oecuménique," *Bulletin d'Orientation Oecuménique,* nn. 23–24, p. 12.

ganized by the councils and the patriarchs. Rome did not intervene, except when called upon, when general ties of intercommunion demanded it or when reference to faith and the universal life of the Church necessitated it. Since the East was internally autonomous, and since her ethos and polity were long separated from Western political influence, she organized and developed her ecclesiological life in conformity with ethnic and cultural realities particular to her own history.

From an ethnic and cultural viewpoint the East achieved a synthesis of Neo-Platonic Hellenism and the existential, concrete Semitic spirit. In Egypt, there is a very striking contrast between the Alexandria of the Fathers and the simple life of the Fathers of the Desert. This synthesis developed especially in Syria, the crossroads of peoples and cultures; from there it spread to Constantinople which owes so much to Antioch. Constantinople assimilated and centralized all the cultural riches of the East. The open and ecumenical Oriental current continued historically in Byzantine Orthodoxy, while the Armenian, Syrian, and Coptic (Egyptian) Churches, dissidents in the Empire, developed mostly along national lines. The Uniate communities historically flow from Orthodoxy; having become minorities in the Roman communion, they were more or less subjected to a Latin spiritual influence.

History ultimately gave the East its own physiognomy. The Orient had not known, as did the West, the upheaval which marked the beginning of the medieval period; the prolongation of the Roman world in the Byzantine world, up to the beginning of the Modern Era, gave the East a sense of continuity and a respect for tradition.

The East was not subjected to the significant transformation of the West by Scholasticism, a scientific and Car-

tesian spirit, a Counter-Reformation, and incredulity. In
many respects, things remained the same as they were
in antiquity. A westerner of the fifth or even of the tenth
century returning to this earth would find himself, in
many ways, less a stranger in the East than in the West.

The Church in the East has not known any clear-cut
freedom with regard to princes, for the Christian princes
had meddled too much in the juridical and disciplinary
aspects of the Church, and Moslem princes allowed her no
freedom to act in temporal or human affairs.

All these elements contributed to the particular traits of
the Eastern church, especially to Orthodoxy. From an ecclesiological point of view, this meant primacy given to the
local church, insistence on the role of a collegial episcopate
in the church, and the participation of the laity in church
life. From a theological point of view, it meant a certain
distrust of the rational, the Euclidean, and of too rigid
juridical thinking and casuistry, as well as an abhorrence
for definitions and systematizations. From a pastoral standpoint it meant failure in social and political life. Spirituality
was mostly contemplative; as a result, there were few, if
any, Oriental saints who were men of action. The predomi-
nance of monasticism together with the prestige of monks
—at times at the expense of the hierarchy—also characterized the Oriental Church.

Religious life in the Orient today centers in the liturgy.
The people do not know any private devotions; it is in the
communal participation in liturgical services, always solemn, that they find nourishment for their faith and spiritual life. The dominant notes of Oriental piety are: humble
compunction, the adoration and praise of the Blessed Trinity, the joyous celebration of the Paschal Mystery every
Sunday, a tender devotion, but without affectation, to the

Mother of God never separated from Her Son, and a profound sense of the sacred.

"The image of Christ, which is at the heart of every Christian denomination, can bear only faint resemblance to the original, and two Christian communities, having the same faith and doctrine, can have ideas which, although essentially the same, are accidentally different enough to appear to be in mutual opposition. Thus Oriental Christianity differs from the western, even in questions where they hardly differ. This is due to innumerable subtleties which defy all attempts at expression."[2]

DOES THE ORIENT HAVE ITS PLACE IN THE CHURCH?

The Oriental Church possesses, first of all, local value, for it was established historically and hierarchically in the vast regions which extend from central Europe to India and Abyssinia. She has enlisted these nations for Christ, has fed them and trained them; she has preserved the Christian name in these countries, despite historical vicissitudes. The missionaries, who came to serve these nations, were sent there, says Benedict XIV, to serve the local hierarchy; they were expected to integrate themselves with that church, to help it *from within* to revivify its institutions, to promote the value of its treasures, and to adapt it to modern conditions consistent with its own traditions. The attachment of almost all the missionaries to a Latin hierarchy, which tried to erect itself at the expense of the Oriental Church, was an anomaly. Whoever is interested in the fate of Christianity in these regions susceptible to Latin influence must hasten to know and love the ven-

2. Bishop André Szepticky, Ruthenian Archbishop of Lvov, in *Commonweal*, (October 8, 1930), p. 570.

erable Christendom of the East. This is the heart of the
missionary spirit, if not of Ecumenism.[3]

The Oriental Church must remain and be respected,
not only for the sake of the East itself, but for the sake of
the Universal Church. "The dignity of the Oriental
churches," says Leo XIII,[4] "consecrated by the most ancient and the most illustrious monuments of history, is in
honor and veneration throughout the entire Christian uni-
verse. Within their bosom, in fact, the first seeds of our
Redemption, gift of Divine Mercy and Providence, have so
rapidly developed that the glories of the apostolate, of
martyrdom, of science and of holiness glowed with their
first splendor and spread their first fruits of salvation and
of joy. From their bosom these great and powerful gifts
flowed to all nations in faraway places. The preservation
of Eastern rites is more important than one might believe.
The august antiquity, which ennobles these diverse rites,
is the ornament of the whole Church, and affirms the divine unity of the Catholic faith. It most clearly shows the
principal Churches of the East their Apostolic origin, and
at the same time focuses the light on their intimate union
with the Church of Rome, which flows from the very principle of Christianity. In fact, nothing better demonstrates
the note of catholicity in the Church of God than the
singular homage of these ceremonies of different forms,
celebrated in languages venerated by antiquity, further
consecrated by the usage made of them by the Apostles
and the Fathers." If the church of the East were to disappear or be absorbed by the Latin Church of the West,

3. I know of a few orphanages in Beirut conducted by French
nuns who educate their students well, but the latter have forgotten
their mother tongue; what might be said of their rite!
4. Encyclical, *Orientalium Dignitas*, 1894.

a great bridge between the contemporary Church and its origins would be destroyed. The church of the East tests the apostolicity of the Church. Moreover, since the Western Church, is a pre-medieval type, she often rediscovers in it her past. In the administrative and spiritual orders, the Oriental Church has in the past, developed values complementary to those stressed in the West. Today the living example of the East is a great help and light to those in the West who work toward spiritual renewal within the meaning of tradition, liturgy, Paschal Mystery, adoration, and lay participation in the life of the Church. Even after the First Vatican Council the Orient shows us the possibility of a decentralized Christianity, as expressed in a local church and in an episcopate organized around a center. The episcopate cannot be a real power next to the papacy—for both are two complementary and necessary realities—unless it is organized on a provincial plan, and unless we return to the metropolitan and the provincial council their effective value.

The Eastern Church also offers us the possibilities of a liturgy and a discipline which are not necessarily unique, but which are capable of being adapted to different races and cultures. The Orient will be a guiding star for Christian communities in Africa and Asia. It shows these nations that Christianity is not a product of the West; that there is a Christianity of the East. After all, Christianity started in the East and accommodated itself to all cultures. During this period of violent reaction against the West, if we want to present Catholicism devoid of its Western context, would it not be fitting to return the Orient to its traditional place in the Church and to utilize its missionary potential? The Orient remains as a sign of the true catholicity of the Church. This great role of the Orient is unfortunately shackled by the schism which separates it from Rome.

WHAT IS THE EASTERN SCHISM?

The separation of the Nestorian and Monophysite Churches can be directly attributed to a refusal to adhere to the Councils of Ephesus and Chalcedon. Therein lies more than one schism. In a return to a general communion, it would be necessary to face up to the problem of their relations not only with Rome, but also with the Byzantine world. Two of their churches were born of an internal split between the patriarchs of Alexandria and Antioch.

But what is the nature of the split which separates the Byzantine East and Rome? This is the schism referred to when one speaks simply of the Eastern Schism. This schism is not the same as the great schism of the West in the fourteenth century; nor is it an act of precise and singular rebellion performed by an individual, but is rather the result of an accepted historical situation which has called into play the complex reality of a collective responsibility. The Eastern Schism cannot be explained by the schism of Photius or of Cerularius. It started before Photius, and many contributing factors of intercommunion persisted long after Cerularius.

Dogmatically and canonically, the schism consists of a refusal to submit to the authority of the Apostolic See of Rome, center of unity and touchstone of the community of the Church. In this sense, Rome, by definition, cannot be schismatic. The schism lies in the local church, and this is why the Greeks, and not the Latins, are called schismatics.

But in the historical reality known as the Eastern Schism, the faults were not all on one side. Father Congar offers this enlightening distinction: "Briefly, the 'schism' appears to us as the acceptance of a situation by which each part of Christendom lives, behaves and judges without taking notice one of the other. We may call it geographical remoteness, provincialism, lack of contact, a 'state of reciprocal ignorance,' alienation, or by the German word 'Entfremdung.' The English word 'estrangement' expresses all this admirably. The Oriental schism came about by a progressive estrangement. . . ."[5]

After a period of life in common, despite diversity, the circumstances which we have analyzed in the previous chapter led the two worlds to isolate themselves and to make an absolute of their own tradition. The error was on the Catholic side in "reconciling a Latinism in fact with a catholicity of intention; there is the danger of practically identifying part of the Christian tradition with that tradition as a whole, and this in the matter of piety and theological thought. We say 'a part of the Christian tradition,' and mean by this not its Western form alone but a period of that tradition—for example its scholastic or medieval or baroque period, or its period of administrative centralization, or similar instances. It is quite a natural tendency to mistake 'accepted' ideas for tradition!

"On the part of the orientals, or more precisely the Orthodox, the danger lies in identifying true Christianity with the Orthodox Church, not only dogmatically but with its national and Eastern forms as such. The conscience of Christianity tends to be identified with the conscience of the East itself. . . ."[6]

5. Yves Congar, *op. cit.*, p. 5.
6. Yves Congar, *op. cit.*, pp. 45–46.

The tragedy was that "the enormous eastern world lived its life without a care for Rome, and without Rome being concerned whether she was considered and loved by it."[7]

The Orient did not want to accept history and welcome the new Western world, and Rome forgot about the East and ancient tradition; she was so much part of the West that the pope was unable to exercise his role as Head of the Church in a way to transcend the duality of East and West. The theological gap between the two worlds was particularly evident in the West, which did not see fit to integrate the patristic and oriental viewpoint, and to arrive at a theology which would be psychologically acceptable to the East, and an ecclesiology which would give the East its traditional place.

Be that as it may, "the responsibilities were shared" and we cannot measure the exact responsibility of the two Churches. However, the Roman pontiff is the first one responsible for the unity of the Church. It is his appropriate function, and since he initiates the call to unity, he must remove the obstacles which, on the part of the papacy and the West have caused the schism; the East will then have to do its own internal work, in which we shall assist her with tact and understanding.

CONDITIONS OF A TRUE DIALOGUE

The West—this book is addressed to Westerners—will have to dissolve the *estrangement*; a better understanding of the East must penetrate the mass of Westerners and must find expression in catechisms and textbooks of Church history, and in theology and canon law in order

7. P. R. Regamey, *Maison-Dieu*, No. 26 (1951–52), p. 159.

that the East be always present on the Western horizon.
Theologians will have to be trained with a view more in
harmony with patristic and Oriental theology without re-
jecting the dogmatic progress realized in the West. Biblical
liturgical and patristic renewal, and progress in Church
history are already contributing to the reduction of the
estrangement.

The papacy will require a respect for Oriental personalities and values, for rites in their full scope, and for patriarchal powers. We have heard Leo XIII take solemn oaths,
in his own name and in behalf of his successors,[8] to the
effect that the preservation of the Oriental reality is not a
question of opportunity but it is a matter of Apostolic value
which popes cannot morally abolish. The behavior of the
papacy toward the united oriental churches is a test, for
the Orthodox, of the value of these promises. It follows,
therefore, that since the entire episcopate at the council
joins the papacy in its promises, the Oriental Church
should be returned to its just place in the Universal
Church. Thus, the complex of mistrust, which leads the
Orthodox to ignore all papal appeals, will vanish. They
will then be able to visualize more sympathetically unity
with the true papal Rome which disassociates general inter-
ests of the Church from those of the Western patriarchate.
Uniatism will then have been an apprenticeship for the
popes.

I cannot offer any better conclusion than the one given

8. In his encyclical *Praeclara Gratulationis* he states: "Nor is there
any reason for you to fear on that account that We or any of Our
successors will ever diminish your rights, the privileges of your patriarchs, or the established ritual of any of your churches. It has been
and always will be the intent and tradition of the Apostolic See, to
make a large allowance, in all that is right and good, for the primitive
traditions and special customs of every nation."

by Father Congar, at the end of his study, which has already been quoted several times: "The advances made to the East from the Catholic side in modern times, seem to be dominated by the sincere desire to *respect* the Eastern churches in their own *rites*. The documents promising the East respect and enjoining the Latins to this respect, have been extremely numerous, especially in the past century. The papacy seems to have considered the problem of reunion as that of a double and reciprocal recognition; the recognition by the papacy of the rights and canonical practices of the Orientals, their recognition of the traditional primacy of the Roman See. On the part of Rome, it would seem that everything could be summed up as follows: We respect and shall respect your rites and your discipline; there is no reason why you should not come back to us.

"It seems to us that these conditions are fair, but only if they are taken with full seriousness and with all their deepest implications. Neither the rites nor the primacy can be reduced to a purely canonical and external question. We are dealing with extremely profound realities, varying though they be in importance, and coming to us from God by different paths. But on both sides there must be acceptance of things as they are: acceptance of the East as the East, acceptance of Rome and the West as the West and as Rome. This amounts to recognizing the inalterable conditions of unity which, providentially, are especially borne by Rome, and also recognizing the full diversity which, under God's Providence, is offered the Church under the species of the duality of an Eastern and a Western Christendom.

"On the part of the East, there is need of an open-mindedness towards what is irreversible in the development of the theological theory of the Church, and in the fact of the primacy: not necessarily the primacy in all the modalities it has been made to take on by history, or even in its present-day form, for a great portion of these elements are of relative and historical order; but a papacy in that minimal form compatible with a local ecclesiastical autonomy such as Photius acknowledged under Nicholas I, and the Bulgarians under Innocent III, and which Innocent IV still found the Greeks ready to accept. This presupposes the successful completion of a vast amount of ecclesiological, biblical and historical work.

"On the part of the West and Rome, it all comes back to their accepting *in truth* the existence of an East, with its own mentality, its genius, its temperament, and its history, and the right it has to be known, accepted and loved for what it is. How good it is to be able to write with A. d'Avril: 'We must not let the Orientals believe that they are tolerated, with their diversities, as an annoying necessity; no, the Catholic Church loves them for themselves, for what they are, and she would not want them to be otherwise.' This, of course, must be entirely true if it is to have real validity. It is easy enough to say: 'Let the Orthodox realize that the return towards Rome does not imply the renunciation of any element of their legitimate tradition'; but there is only one way for them to realize this, namely, that it be true; and the means for making it be true, is for us to believe in it, and to have no other desire in our hearts. The Orientals are never fooled as to our feelings for them; they appreciate every sign of *real* respect and if such signs were to increase, the complex of distrust which shuts all the doors, would surely vanish before long. For this, the scientific studies that have been pursued for several decades in the Catholic Church under the very powerful encouragement of the papacy, through the Assumptionist Fathers or the Pontifical Oriental Institute, are of inestimable value. Necessary as they are as preliminaries to a better understanding of things, these studies are, nonetheless, merely preliminaries. Even the rather general revival of interest in the Greek patristic sources of Christian life and thought, as evidenced by Father Daniélou and the French collection, *Sources Chrétiennes*, must be counted also on the level of preparations. We must hope that, thanks to all this and beyond all this, a true sympathy and a warm esteem for the Christian East will enter into the living tissue of Latin Catholicism.

"Thus a general rapprochement is the indispensable preparation for a reunion. No doubt, one of the causes of the failure of past advances and efforts was the lack of psychological preparation on *both sides*. A reunion should not merely be discussed and decreed. If the historical process of the schism was a gradual and general estrangement, and if in substance it consists in the acceptance of a situation of non-rapport, then the reunion, which should be the cure of the schism, can only be the result of a resumption of contacts full of esteem and sympathy—two words that really stand for charity. Adopting the expression of a German author we have cited before, we can say that there will be no *'Wiedervereinigung'* (reunion) without long, patient, intelligent and loving *'Wiederbegegnung'* (renewal of contact). The actual means are not hard to imagine: what the heart desires, the mind will invent. Before arguing on the points of divergency, and especially before seeking union by way of canonical or diplomatic dealings, a psychological and spiritual reconciliation must be sought and feelings of confidence, and of real sympathy, aroused. This can only be done by converting into actual fact to the highest degree, and, if it be necessary, emphasizing the mutual affinity of the two churches—or, if needs be, by recreating it. We have borrowed the phrase 'mutual affinity' from an Anglican writer, just as we have borrowed the word 'estrangement' from the English, thus proving that we can learn from those with whom we often disagree.

"The Churches of the East and the West have an affinity between them that goes much deeper than their estrangement. The Orthodox are well aware of it, and some of them, not the least eminent in their Church, have told us that in their ecumenical conferences they felt they were also speaking for the Catholic Church. The differences will tend to grow in the same measure that they are not respected; similarly, if they are recognized for what they are, the profound affinities between the Churches will assert themselves and the chance for reunion will be strengthened. At the same time, the serious reasons which contribute towards a favorable reconsideration or interpretation of the disputed questions will be freed from the burden of the distrust which prevents them from exerting all their force. In any case, no matter how efficacious the visible results, one worthwhile consequence will at least have been attained: the spirit of schism will no longer be able to claim a place in our hearts.

"We repeat: dogmatically and canonically, the main factor in the Oriental schism is the refusal to submit to the primacy of the Roman See; actually and historically, the schism is the result of a gradual and general estrangement. Not that the schism is of itself the estrangement; rather the schism is the acceptance of the estrangement. The sin of schism is already committed in the heart when we behave as though we were not an integral part of the whole with others, *alter alterius membra* (Rom. 12,5). In this organic whole which is the Church, each local church not only realizes the mystical nature of the whole, mainly through the sacramental life, but is itself also *a part* of that whole, according to the plan of God which is to assemble all mankind into one Church and to represent, in the catholicity of that Church, the infinite riches of His gifts. If the Church is like a body, of which the East and the West are, we might say, the two sides, Rome is the visible head of the body, for the purpose of regulating its movements as a unity. To accept each other really means that each accept the other acording to the role that each is to play in the total organism; it means that each one accepts the other as members of the same body, according to the vocation and function that is assigned to each part.

"Depending upon the dogmatic and canonical reality of non-submission to, or acceptance of, the Head, the schism is made or abolished at a single blow. The actual acceptance of the estrangement, according to history, had begun long before the year 1054; but it has not been completed so long as there exist, here and there, people who do not share the feeling of estrangement. We contribute to the schism, even today, whenever we assume the attitudes of estrangement, or when we accept the results of many centuries of alienation; we continue it every time we commit, even today, acts analogous to those, positive or negative, which in the past made evident a lack of union. On the other hand, we contribute towards ending the schism and actually end it, to the extent that it exists in us, by every act or attitude of ours which rejects and weakens that estrangement. Every time we recognize the existence of the East, and the East recognizes the existence of Rome and the West, to that extent, the wound has been healed."[9]

9. Yves Congar, *op. cit.*, pp. 85–90.

A NOTE ON THE TYPE

IN WHICH THIS BOOK IS SET

This book is set in Fairfield, a Linotype face, created by Rudolph Ruzicka, distinguished American artist and engraver. Introduced in 1940, Fairfield is almost strictly a book type with much charm and beauty. It is easy to read as one learns from extensive reading, since it furnishes some degree of stimulation and pleasure to the eye. The fitting of each letter is practically perfect, which is a real tribute to its designer. This book was composed by Progressive Typographers, Inc., of York, Pa., printed by the Wickersham Printing Company of Lancaster, Pa. and bound by Moore and Company of Baltimore, Md. The typography and design are by Howard N. King.